Please **RETURN** or **RENEW**
no later than the date on the receipt
Subject to recall if requested

LONG LOAN

University of Stirling Libr...
Tel: 01786 46...

DI313494

3213144500

Acknowledgements

I am indebted to the encouragement and advice of all the members of the Seven Million advisory group, including: Professor Ray Pahl, a sociologist from the University of Canterbury; Phil Ward, Group Personnel Executive, Northern Foods; David May, Head of Equal Opportunities, NatWest; Victoria Hillier, Head of Equal Opportunities, British Telecom; Sandra Sanglin, Social Policy Manager, IBM (UK); Tony Allen, Human Resources Partner, Coopers and Lybrand; Lesley Holland, Corporate Equality Adviser, BBC and Jan Hall, Chief Executive of Gold Greenlees Trott. I owe special thanks to Pat Dade, Director of Synergy Brand Values for providing unlimited access to the data from Insight '94, for helping me to analyse it and for his permission to publish it in this report. I am also grateful to Jo Gardiner, Campaign Manager of The Industrial Society and Martin LeJeune, Head of Public Policy Unit, NatWest, for their comments on a draft of the report. Finally, I would like to thank Daniel Oren Sabbagh for his help with the footnotes and his painstaking fact checking. Naturally, the usual disclaimers apply.

No Turning Back:

generations and the genderquake

Helen Wilkinson

DEM⊙S

First published in 1994
by
Demos
9 Bridewell Place
London EC4V 6AP
tel: 071 353 4479
fax: 071 353 4481

Paper No. 10

ISBN 1 898 309 75 2

Cover design by Adrian Taylor

Printed in Great Britain by
White Dove Press
London
Typesetting by Bartle & Wade Associates

CONTENTS

Introduction

Throughout the Western world old certainties in work and family life are disappearing. Traditional definitions of what it means to be a man or a woman are fading. One reaction to these changes is despair, and there is no shortage of people warning of imminent moral and societal breakdown. Many are looking for someone or something to blame, whether it be single mothers, feckless fathers or the legacy of the 1960s. But the real issue behind much of the renewed concern about the family and community is if anything simpler than they suggest. It is that we are in the middle of an historic change in the relations between men and women: a shift in power and values that is unravelling many of the assumptions not only of 200 years of industrial society, but also of millennia of traditions and beliefs.

This book is about the people who are at the forefront of this change; the over seven million women and over seven million men[1] between the ages of 18 and 34 in the UK, who account for just under a third of the voting population. It focuses primarily on their values - and how these differ from previous generations - and it reflects their optimism that however disorienting change may be, its balance is mainly positive. The book makes seven central arguments:

• first, that the cultural and economic enfranchisement of women is deep-rooted and irreversible. The desire for autonomy and self-fulfilment, through work as much as family; the valuing of risk, excitement and change; and the convergence of values of young men and women, all suggest a significant, and deepening, contrast with the values of an older generation. Contrary to the popular belief that values swing like a pendulum between left and right, tradition and progress, liberalism and authoritarianism, most of the important changes in values are cumulative in nature.

• second, that although changes of such magnitudes have many sources, two great drivers stand out. One is the economy - the combination of women's greater preparedness to take on part-time and service jobs and firms' rising demand for the adaptability, dexterity and skill in services that they believe women can offer. The other is culture and aspiration: women's growing desire for greater autonomy and the chance to develop identities through work.

• third, that although the direction of change is unmistakeable it is uneven across regions and class, and involves strong negative reactions amongst some groups of men. These reactions need to be understood sympathetically, not dismissed. We need to acknowledge that the solution of old problems is highlighting new ones: such as how to replace women's informal labour in the home, how to finance childcare and eldercare of sufficiently high quality, or how to find useful roles for unskilled men, whose traditional jobs in construction, manufacturing and the army have contracted sharply.

• fourth, that the advance of women in our culture and parts of the economy is shifting the terms of the debate away from the assumptions both of defenders of more traditional values and of an earlier generation of feminists. An older agenda of rights, that saw relations between men and women as a zero sum game, is being superseded by a much more complex set of issues: overwork for some and underwork for others; discrimination against men as well as women; sexual harassment by women as well as men; coping with the cultural barriers to male adaptation as well as the remaining barriers to women.

• fifth, that politics is lagging behind. Traditional political parties and what were once new women's organisations are failing to reflect the concerns of a new generation. The main parties have fewer than one in twenty members under 25. Nearly half of 18-25 year olds did not vote in 1992. A younger generation has absorbed much of the feminist argument but no longer identifies either with the feminist label or with women's organisations.

• sixth, that policy-makers need to bridge the generation gap. The party which can capture the imagination and support of the seven million generation will in the long run stand to benefit enormously, just as those businesses, brands and campaigns that can resonate with the ethos of this generation will gain an invaluable and dynamic competitive advantage.

• seventh, that a new agenda is needed which fits the values and concerns of the seven million generation - redefining the balance between rights, freedoms and responsibilities, rethinking male roles in a changed economic climate, providing more supportive structures for individuals to make choices about work, care and parenting, and updating equality strategies to embrace diversity as well as guaranteeing rights.

This book, and the project of which it is a part, have focused on the seven million generation for a simple reason: their views have so far been absent from public debates about the family and community. These are dominated by mainly male, middle-aged decision-makers and commentators. Most female commentators are a generation older than those they write about. Younger women in particular have remarkably few national representatives and few representatives in Parliament (indeed there is only one in the age group[2]). This book redresses that imbalance and fills the gap.

Geoff Mulgan, Director of Demos

PART ONE:
The Background: Changing values

- The British Value Map

With peace and steady growth British values have changed substantially over the last quarter century. These shifts have been mapped by Synergy, a market research company which has used representative samples of 2,500 people, over a period of 20 years, to analyse how values have changed.[3] The story they tell is a complex one, but it has a number of key themes which provide the background to any serious analysis of the direction of change in British society. The map opposite shows the current basic pattern of values using cluster analysis to show which values tend to group together. *(Synergy's work, and the methodology used, are explained more fully in the appendix).*

The first theme is that there has been a long-run swing away from traditional concerns for security, authority, rigid moral codes and a belief in the centrality of the family, that dominated the value map a generation ago. Today these cluster in the top left-hand corner of the map. They have become less central for two main reasons. One is that the combination of economic growth and a welfare state has largely met most people's basic, 'sustenance-driven' needs. The second is that there has been a deep-seated weakening of tradition throughout society and culture. A significant minority, mainly over 55, still holds these traditional values, and related values such as consumer-scepticism and a parochial attachment to neighbourhood. But, as the map shows, amongst the majority of the population these values have now moved to the periphery.

The second big trend has been the rise of what could be called outer-directed values concerned with status, image and consumption, which cluster in the bottom left-hand corner.

4

British Values '94

all ages

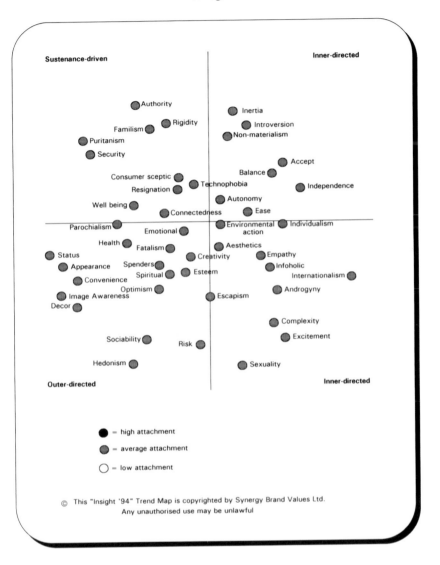

Sustenance-driven

Inner-directed

Authority

Inertia

Rigidity

Introversion

Familism

Non-materialism

Puritanism

Security

Accept

Balance

Consumer sceptic

Technophobia

Independence

Resignation

Autonomy

Well being

Ease

Connectedness

Parochialism

Environmental action

Individualism

Emotional

Health

Aesthetics

Fatalism

Status

Empathy

Appearance

Creativity

Infoholic

Spenders

Esteem

Convenience

Spiritual

Internationalism

Optimism

Image Awareness

Escapism

Androgyny

Decor

Complexity

Excitement

Sociability

Risk

Hedonism

Sexuality

Outer-directed

Inner-directed

● = high attachment

◕ = average attachment

○ = low attachment

These came to dominate society and politics in the 1970s and 1980s, and were effectively represented by the Conservatives as they transcended the conventional class boundaries of British politics by tapping into a culture of aspiration. They remain significant for a substantial number of people of all ages.

But today, in the 1990s, the value map of British society has changed again. A substantial group has moved beyond outer-directed values towards more innerdirected ones, such as empathy, connectedness, emotion, autonomy, ease and green concerns. These signal a shift away from the concern with the outer trappings of success. 30 years ago they were on the periphery, but today these values cluster at the centre of the map, showing that they have become mainstream in the 1990s.

These shifts from sustenance-driven values, through outer-directed to innerdirected, affect every area of behaviour. For example, those in the first group might have children because of traditional moral values, those in the second because it fits their image of success or normality, those in the third group because they seek the quality of the parenting experience.

The map also gives us some indication of where values may be shifting. The leading edge values, which are now moving from the periphery towards the centre, include androgyny (the blurring of gender difference), internationalism and balance, complexity and excitement.

In general the long-term shifts can best be understood in terms of a deepening of attachment to autonomy. But over time the meaning of autonomy has gradually changed. As people gain more freedom over their own lives few remain satisfied with a narrowly selfish version of autonomy. Instead, as the map shows, people also seek new forms of belonging, experience or attachment as the corollary of their enhanced freedom.

- The values of British women

Women have been at the forefront of these changes: their values have changed most and have come to define the overall shape of British values, so that today they tend to score above average on the central values of society. Although on the whole women are still more attached than men to the family and authority (perhaps because at home they still bear a heavier responsibility for maintaining order) there are clear signs of a movement away from rigid moral codes and puritanical values. As a group their values are becoming androgynous; they are much more willing than men are to think flexibly about gender roles. *(See value map on the next page).*

Amongst women as a whole, it is working women (and particularly those with higher education, and those committed to careers) who are setting the pace. They have higher self-esteem than non-working women, and are becoming more escapist, more internationalist, more inclined to take risks and be hedonistic, and more at ease with complexity than women without jobs. By comparison with the past, and despite recession, they are relatively unconcerned about financial security.[4]

This map reinforces previous data about the extent to which women's attitudes to work and family have changed. For example a report by the National Council for Women published two years ago[5] found remarkable changes in attitudes to parenting. While 21% of the women wanted to spend more time with their families, only 13% of women of child-bearing age thought that children were necessary to feel fulfilled. 29% wanted more time for education and 47% more time for hobbies. 50% of women aged between 16 and 54 said that more equal sharing of home roles was a priority for the future.

British Women '94

all ages

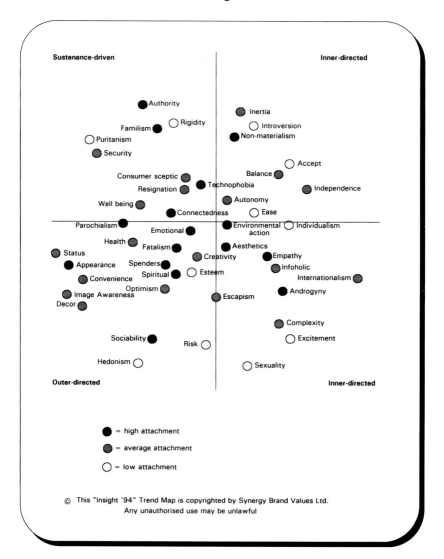

Note: The value map of British Men '94 (*all ages*) is a mirror of this map i.e. where women are shown to have high attachments on this map men have correspondingly lower attachments.

In general these maps confirm that British values have been **feminised** in two important ways. First because women are leading the process of value changes and second because the core values can more readily be identified as 'feminine'.

- Social drivers of change

Changing values reflect innumerable sources. One obvious factor behind the feminisation of attitudes, and the strong attachment amongst women to autonomy, is the remarkable influence, both direct and indirect, of the women's movement. The legal changes women's organisations and the women's liberation movement have campaigned for have had cumulative effects: the passage of the 1967 abortion act; the outlawing of sexual discrimination and equal pay legislation all reinforced the principle of gender equity.

Advances in medical technology have also played a part and now enable women to exercise reproductive choice well beyond the 'choice' of abortion. Sperm banks, the option of artificial insemination and, in the years ahead, the vastly greater potential choice offered by genetics, are all enabling increasing numbers of women to control their own destiny and the terms on which they have children.

In our culture as a whole, women have become more visible and more assertive. In many respects through figures like Sigourney Weaver and Madonna, kd lang and Sharon Stone, popular culture has been far ahead of politics in thinking through the blurring of the boundaries of male and female identity, and the potency of female sexuality. Soap operas have been as significant a medium as any in publicly working through changing roles.[6] Elsewhere too, the role models for women and girls are no longer passively feminine: Joanna Lumley in 'Absolutely Fabulous', Helen Mirren in 'Prime Suspect' and Imogen Stubbs in 'Anna Lee' all play strong, independent women succeeding in a man's world on their own terms.[7] Feminist ideas, from psychology and history to philosophy and even theology, have seeped almost subliminally into the mainstream.

- Economics as a driver of change

Most of these changes in culture and ideas have been built around the assertion of women's rights. But need has also been a driver of change, as powerful economic forces have created new opportunities for women to work, so enabling them to take part in what has become the dominant source of status and identity in modern Western societies. The key facts are these:

• The participation of women between the ages of 16 and 64 has risen from 53% in 1973 to 65% in 1991. Male participation dropped from 93% to 86% in the same period and in the last 15 years 2 million men have disappeared from the workforce.[8] In some parts of the country women employees now outnumber men,[9] and most forecasters expect this to be true nationwide by the end of the century.[10]

• The female/male gap in earnings has narrowed, although it remains substantial. According to one measure (the New Earnings Survey) the ratio rose from 63% in 1972 to 73% in 1976, and reached 79% in 1991. According to the broader General Household Survey the ratio rose from 62% in the late 1970s to 67% in the late 1980s.

• Across all parts of the earnings distribution women's share in household income has risen. The sharpest rise in women's employment has been among graduates. Employment of women of intermediate and lower educational levels has also increased. The only exceptions are at the bottom of the earnings scale where the benefits system disincentivises work for women whose partners are unemployed, and where lower pay for unskilled male partners has cut family incomes and indirectly undermined women's economic empowerment.[11] Over the last 20 years women's share in household incomes has risen from a quarter to one third.[12]

• There has been a steady rise in part-time work, where women make up 85% of the workforce. In the last decade part-time work amongst women has increased from over 4 million to just over 5 million.[13]

• Women's self-employment is steadily growing, after only a short recessionary pause. There are now about 750,000 self-employed women in the UK, and rising numbers starting their own businesses, mirroring trends in the USA.[14]

• More women are entering into professions previously seen as male preserves. Medicine and dentistry are two examples. Women now account for 54% of newly qualified solicitors - an increase of almost 9% over the last seven years - and 37% of the new intake of chartered accountants are female - an increase of over 10% in the last decade.[15] Women account for 38% of professional jobs (forecast to be the highest growth occupational group over the next ten years), and their share of 'corporate managers and administrators' rose from 11% in 1979 to 19% in 1989.[16]

• Women's power as consumers is evolving rapidly, shifting away from utilitarian purchasing for the home to consumption that is more closely tied to identity. For example women's rising consumption of cars[17] is encouraging a quite new set of advertising images, some ostentatiously asserting women's independence of men (although, interestingly, virtually no women are involved in the design of cars).[18]

Many of these shifts would have been impossible if women's expectations had not changed. But, equally, they are not comprehensible except in the context of deep structural changes in the economy away from manufacturing.[19]

Since 1950 five million jobs in the UK have gone from goods producing industries, while about eight million jobs have been created in services, which have tended to be more open to women.[20] As we shall see the growth areas have been jobs in care, in interpersonal services, and in part-time, less secure jobs generally; all fields where women have predominated. As a result most forecasters now predict that women will take 80-90% of new jobs in the next few years.[21]

- Feminisation at work

In the past politics and law were seen as the main ways of improving the status of women in the labour market. The UK courts interpretation of EU directives on equal pay, which has significantly improved part-timers rights (in the teeth of UK government opposition which argues that the effect will be to reduce employment opportunities)[22] is only the most recent example.

But changes are now coming as much from internal pressures: from shifts in technology, industry structures and ways of organising. These go far beyond quantitative shifts in employment patterns and amount to a deeper feminisation of the economy. Employers increasingly want a more flexible and dextrous workforce - attributes associated much more with women than men. Jobs requiring physical strength - in the army, construction and parts of manufacturing - are in decline. Many of the long-term growth areas, both in private and public services, rely on caring skills and the ability to cope well with face to face interactions. For example jobs in community, social and personal services rose 3.5m between 1950 and 1990, and even public service jobs increased by 1.25m during the Thatcherite 1980s.[23]

For employers, flexibility (a word fraught with ambiguities) is the key. 80% of large companies already employ temporary or part-time workers, 65% contract out work and 60% use flexible working patterns. By 1997 over three-quarters of large companies expect the use of flexible working amongst their permanent staff to increase, three-quarters predict an increase in the contracting out of work and two thirds say they will use more temporary workers to supplement the existing workforce. 11% of large employers currently employ teleworkers whilst 22% employ homeworkers.[24]

As Robert Reich, the US Labor Secretary said at a recent Guardian seminar in London the effect of these shifts in working patterns is to feminise the very language of work. The qualities that used to be associated with women's work - flexibility, adaptability, service and teamwork - are now being demanded of men.[25] Discontinuous and uncertain work is becoming far more widespread. Moreover, as security increasingly comes from employability in a fluid labour market rather than from having a permanent job[26] women appear to be better prepared, culturally and psychologically.[27]

In the past feminisation and flexibility were often little more than codewords for low pay and exploitation. Today the move away from traditional work patterns is still being driven by the needs of employers to lower fixed costs and respond more rapidly to fluctuations in demand. Flexibility, and new approaches like the zero hour contracts being introduced in retailing and other fields, can still place additional burdens on-to employees, denying them any job security.[28]

But flexibility can also improve choices for employees. Many actively seek part-time work, and there is now an accumulation of evidence that more full-timers want to go part-time than vice versa.[29] A recent qualitative report on attitudes to part-time work, found that most women choose to work part-time not only as a way of balancing family and work commitments and achieving some financial independence but also as a way of gaining self-esteem.[30]

Some companies are learning to see flexibility and the option of part-time working not only as a way of avoiding costly redundancies but also as a means of enhancing their image as family friendly employers. British Airways is a good example. When under pressure in 1993 to reduce labour costs it offered its employees the option of part-time work and found little problem with take up. Virgin Airways applied a similar strategy with equally positive results.[31] There have been parallel experiences in the public sector. In the Inland Revenue, as an alternative to job cuts, the IRSF negotiated a programme for full-time employees to reduce their working hours, with preference given to parents of young children and those looking after sick or elderly relatives.[32]

Nor is part-time and more flexible working still only to be found in relatively unskilled jobs. Instead it is rising up the hierarchy;[33] according to one recent report, Flexible Working for Managers,[34] seven out of ten blue chip companies now employ part-time managers and over 80% of employers believe that part-time working for managers will become increasingly popular.

Farsighted employers are trying to find ways of making economic necessity fit the changing values of their female workforce[35] so that they can recruit and retain working mothers. Policy innovation and experiment is now intense, whether on **flexibility**: homeworking, job shares, part-time and term-time working, right through to flexi-time or flexi-place working;[36] on **family friendliness**, with everything from workplace creches right through to emergency nanny services;[37] and on **empowerment**: mentoring schemes and women's leadership and development programmes to encourage more women to try for management (schemes which appear not only to benefit the junior women but also those who had to rise without the benefit of supportive networks).[38] Some companies, many of them signatories to Opportunity 2000, have combined initiatives of this kind with **corporate targets** on equal opportunities so as to drive change throughout the organisation. Companies which have already set corporate targets are beginning to think through the next phase of this strategy by encouraging managers to 'own' change by setting them individual targets.

A significant number of businesses still see flexibility solely in terms of cost-reduction, and have been at best half-hearted in understanding the full implications of the changes in values. But as a result of persuasion and experience most large companies are now familiar with arguments stressing the business case for active equal opportunities policies: the benefits not only in terms of recruitment but also in terms of influencing consumers, and indeed all those who may influence their working environment.[39] Increasingly an argument that used to be couched in moral terms (and a language of rights) is being recast in terms of competitive advantage.[40]

- Feminisation and the firm

The feminisation of work processes is being matched by a feminisation of work organisation. In some parts of industry rigid hierarchies of control are giving way to management styles that combine tough control over some parameters (such as finance) with much looser, more team-based approaches. Authors such as Charles Handy have argued that de-layering within organisations will inevitably weaken obstacles such as the glass ceiling. Firms will change from being 'employing' organisations to become 'organising' organisations with a core of key people managing the firm while operational tasks are sub-contracted to businesses and individuals on the periphery selling their services into the organisation. Within the firm feminine values will come to the fore, involving less pyramidal structures, more openness, networking and a higher premium for interpersonal skills.[41] Some business leaders, such as Nick Temple of IBM UK, even speak of the need to accept these more 'feminine' values as a strategic priority. One symptom of this shift is that some firms now recognise the value of signs of a 'hinterland' - a breadth of interests and engagements - in their employees, instead of expecting a complete focus on the employer's needs. Their argument is that this provides more balanced and more efficient employees than a demand for total dedication to work.[42]

Some of these trends are more pronounced than others. There is certainly clearer evidence of the overall shift of the labour market towards women than there is of the softer shifts - the revaluing of part-time work or 'hinterland'. But what is not in doubt is the historic shift away from the old division of labour -between domestic work undertaken by women, and predominantly full-time paid work undertaken by men.[43]

- Adapting through necessity

As waves of change sweep through society the effects are complex, often shaped by the occupational history of different regions and groups. It would be simplistic to argue that all the drivers of change have been felt uniformly. Many men, in particular, have found it difficult to adapt to change - a factor we discuss in more depth later.

Two categories stand out in helping us to understand the way different groups have responded. Some people's values, especially the values of educated women and men, have clearly been shaped by 'rights' arguments for gender equity. But other groups have been driven by a need to experiment with less fixed gender roles, and have adapted their values accordingly. For example many working class women who began working to supplement the family income have come to value work as a source of independent identity in its own right.

Unskilled men, too, have been forced by economic necessity to re-evaluate their roles, and apply for the kinds of service sector jobs which they used to see as 'women's work'.[44] The extent of change was visible in coverage of the tenth anniversary of the miner's strike which was celebrated this year: a classic instance of a male strike in which women played an extremely active, but subordinate role. Ten years on many former miners are working on predominantly female production lines in casualised sweatshops labouring over the fineries of stitching bras, and some have become househusbands while their wives act as breadwinners.

Across the UK, men's groups, previously the preserve of educated 'pro-feminist' men, are being set up in untypical places: on council estates where unemployed men, many of them young, meet for companionship and learn together how to adapt. In one Glasgow council estate, and another in Bristol, we have found men's groups providing home economics classes, classes in cookery and opportunities to share tips on child rearing: almost precisely the functions that many women's groups served in the past. Indeed, in the Glasgow case, the women on the estate have since set up their own group to discuss how they cope with their partners' changed behaviour.[45]

These men, relatively uneducated, many unemployed or used to unskilled labour, are the unlikely personification of 'new man'. Some now expect all work for them in the future to be part-time and insecure.[46] Others even welcome it. Anecdotal evidence collected by the Equal Opportunities Commission suggests that a significant minority of younger men are actively seeking out part-time, temporary jobs so that they can share their children's upbringing.

In recent years the North of England has become one of the fastest areas of change. It is there that the loss of male manufacturing has been most sharply felt, that the relative enfranchisement of women has happened most quickly and that what was previously denigrated as 'women's work' is now being most actively sought, by men and women alike. Perhaps the most telling symbol of the reversal of fortune between Northern men and women is the phenomenon of girls' nights out to the Chippendales, which is spreading in the North as well as the South East, and partially displacing the old habits of male visits to strip clubs. Women's increasing outer-directedness is leading them to display what we used to see as male characteristics. They are unashamedly seeking entertainment and hedonism and there is even anecdotal evidence of professional women using male escorts on business trips in a classic inversion of old gender roles.[47]

PART TWO:
Generation and the genderquake

Taken together, changing attitudes to sexuality, the family, work and life expectations amount to what US author Naomi Wolf has labelled a 'genderquake' in her book *Fire With Fire*; a fundamental shift in power from men to women.[48] But this shift cannot be understood simply as a shift of power. It is also bound up with generational changes in values, as men, particularly younger men, begin to change their attitudes to work, life and leisure, in tandem with women.

This becomes particularly clear when we look at the values of the seven million generation: the seven million men and seven million women between 18 and 34. Women and men entering work at 16 in 1975, the year the Sex Discrimination Act was passed, are now 35. At the other end of the age range, 18 year olds entering work today have not only been acclimatised to the principle of equality in law from an early age, but have also seen women enter the workforce in greater numbers than ever before, confidently filling jobs, some at the very pinnacles of power. These women and men under 34 are the first 'post-equality' cohort, the first generation to come of age since the great battles of the feminist movement in the 1970s and the first to benefit from the achievement of equal opportunities legislation.

- The deepening of value shifts

Amongst the women in this group, we can see a marked **deepening** of the value shifts we described earlier: growing attachment to values such as androgyny, balance, risk, excitement and hedonism. More than any previous generation they are rejecting the whole cluster of traditional values: authority, rigid moral codes of right and wrong, the emphasis on security (financial and otherwise), older parochial notions of community and the puritanism of the past. They are less attached to the family than previous generations at the same age and more likely to feel tied down by it. Amongst working women, especially those interested in careers, these trends are much stronger, and they are also the most optimistic about the future. Graduate, career-minded women are now much less likely to feel the need for a partner, and are more empathic, more green and internationalist, and, in general, more inner-directed in their values.

Other research reinforces the Synergy evidence. 79% of younger women (those aged between 16 and 35) say that they very much want to develop their career at work or find employment, whilst only 50% say that having children, or more children, is a goal. Only 23% of young women (16-24) believe that a woman needs a stable relationship to feel fulfilled.[49] In general, the high fliers in this generation are much less compromising and have much higher (and possibly unrealistic) expectations of their career than older generations.[50] Other research found that a younger generation of women managers were planning their career more consciously than in the past.[51] The Synergy data confirms that even young women aged between 18-34 who work just to earn a living are now strongly attached to work as a source of identity.

These value shifts are, not surprisingly, affecting behaviour. The re-evaluation of the centrality of career and work over the home and family is leading to rising cohabitation and 'postponed pregnancy'. Over half today's 25 year olds have cohabited with a partner compared with 1-2% 25 years ago.[52] On average, women now have their first child at almost 28[53], often so that an identity at work can be established first. The implication is not that this generation has turned against having children but rather that it wants to control parenting and place it within a context of other goals.

Beyond their attachment to work and their rejection of old forms of family and community, something deeper is also happening. Young women are exhibiting what have typically been seen as male attributes - they are less emotional than other women (see the value map over the page) and more willing to take risks and seek excitement in activities such as foreign travel, parachuting or rockclimbing. Attitudes to sexuality are changing. Younger women are now more interested in sexuality than previous generations:[54] one recent survey found that 10% of women aged between 25-34 had had more than 10 partners compared to just 4% in their mothers' generation.[55] This trend of a growing interest in sexuality can be seen particularly clearly amongst today's 15-17 year olds according to the Synergy data and women at 16 are now only 4% less likely to have had sexual intercourse than boys.[56]

The young British woman of today might best be described as facing two ways - on the one hand flirting with power in an outer-directed phase and exhibiting what have hitherto been seen as male characteristics, and on the other hand edging towards more inner-directed values - the attachment to balance and ease.

The cumulative nature of most of these shifts - particularly the leading role of women - seems likely to continue. A sea-change is underway in younger girls' attitudes which is having a direct bearing on educational performance. School girls now have greater self-esteem, are happier than their male peers, are more ambitious, are more likely to want to continue in education and are less likely to want to start a family when they leave school than boys.[57] Above all, perhaps, girls are much more positive about the future than boys - an attitude which clearly has a direct bearing on their willingness to study hard.[58] Girls are now outperforming boys at GCSE level even in so-called 'male' subjects like science. They are outperforming boys at 'A' level, and now outnumber, and are outperforming, men at university. Indeed at university, women have made the greatest strides in science degrees where over the last eight years they have dramatically closed the gap and overtaken men in many

7 Million Women '94

18-34 age group

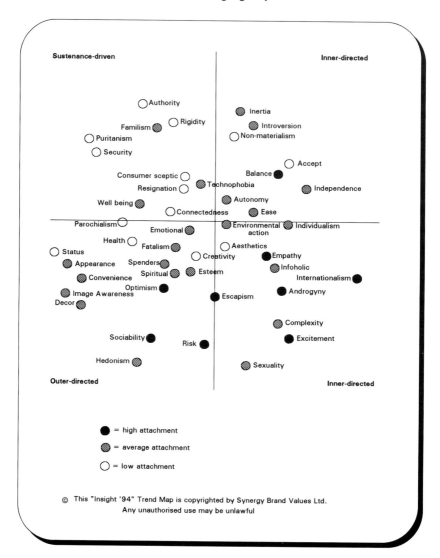

7 Million Men '94
18-34 age group

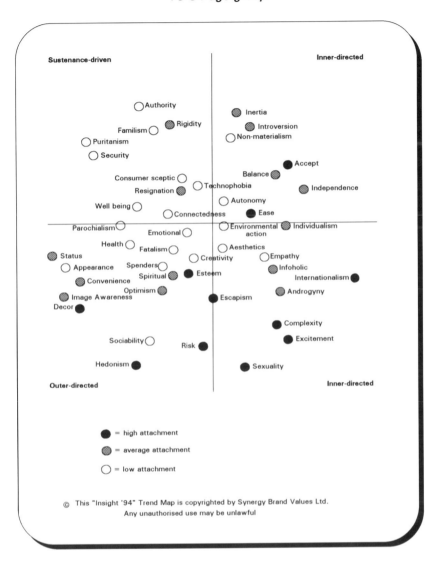

Sustenance-driven

Inner-directed

Authority

Inertia

Rigidity

Introversion

Familism

Non-materialism

Puritanism

Security

Accept

Consumer sceptic

Balance

Technophobia

Independence

Resignation

Autonomy

Well being

Connectedness

Ease

Parochialism

Environmental
action

Individualism

Emotional

Health

Aesthetics

Status

Fatalism

Appearance

Creativity

Empathy

Spenders

Infoholic

Convenience

Spiritual

Esteem

Internationalism

Optimism

Image Awareness

Escapism

Androgyny

Decor

Complexity

Sociability

Excitement

Risk

Hedonism

Sexuality

Outer-directed

Inner-directed

● = high attachment

◍ = average attachment

○ = low attachment

© This "Insight '94" Trend Map is copyrighted by Synergy Brand Values Ltd.
Any unauthorised use may be unlawful

23

areas. As a result they are now less likely than men to be unemployed when they graduate: 8.2% of women graduates are unemployed a year after graduation compared to 12.25% of men.[59]

- Converging Values

While younger women's values diverge from those of their parents and grandparents, they are converging with those of younger men. Their value maps are now remarkably similar, revealing the same shift towards values at the bottom of the map and away from tradition.

One partial exception is that although young men are much more at ease with androgyny than older men, they have still not gone as far as young women. However this now seems to be changing, with a strong attachment to androgyny amongst men under 25, particularly those between the ages of 15-17.

There has also been a convergence in attitudes to equality. One study of teenagers in the early 1990s found overwhelming support for equal opportunities for men and women amongst almost all girls and five-sixths of boys, and although there were differences in attitudes to women's role as mothers, a majority of the young men still disagreed with the proposition that mothers should care for a sick child and that childrearing is a full-time job.[60] Many young men seem to have belatedly absorbed feminist arguments.

In general convergence is most marked amongst the 20-25% of higher educated young men and young women, many of whom strongly value gender equality as a good in itself. One effect of this is that they are attracted to companies with a strong female presence and effective equal opportunities policies: these are taken as markers of being smart and leading-edge. Younger men and women both share a commitment to active leisure pursuits, and seek the kinds of flexible working patterns that can sustain a balanced lifestyle. Both want work to be challenging and interesting, with lots of feedback and validation, and their friendship patterns are becoming more alike.[61]

The cumulative nature of these shifts is confirmed by Synergy's data for 15-17 year olds who are even more attached to the core values of the seven million generation: seeking escapism, risk, excitement, sexuality, hedonism, image awareness and internationalism and rejecting the family, puritanism, and rigidity much more than teenagers in previous decades.

By contrast there is a huge gap in values between the post-equality generation and those over 55 who remain strongly attached to the 'sustenance driven' value cluster. They are more deferential, and more committed to the traditional nuclear family and distinct gender roles, and, perhaps because of unease about the decay of tradition, more pessimistic about the future.

Casual observers of modern British life might expect that geography would be a more important shaper of values than variables like gender or generation. After all, there is still a world of difference between Wigan or Easterhouse and the Home Counties. The Synergy data does indeed confirm that the North remains more attached to sustenance-driven and outer-directed values than the South-East, and more pessimistic about the future. But when the data is broken down by generation a very different picture emerges. Although, as we shall see, there are important exceptions, most young men and women under 34 in the North across all classes are relatively optimistic about the future and at ease with themselves, open to the blurring of gender differences, to sexuality, complexity and risk. In other words, generation is becoming a better predictor of attitudes than class or geography.

7 Million Generation '94

18-34 age group

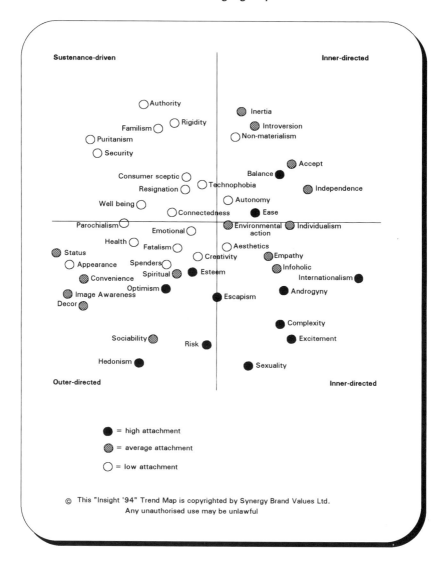

Sustenance-driven

Inner-directed

○ Authority
○ Rigidity
Familism ○
○ Puritanism
○ Security

◉ Inertia
◉ Introversion
○ Non-materialism

◉ Accept
Consumer sceptic ○   Balance ●
Resignation ○   ○ Technophobia   ◉ Independence
Well being ○   ○ Autonomy
○ Connectedness   ● Ease
Parochialism ○   ◉ Environmental   ◉ Individualism
Emotional ○   action
Health ○   ○ Aesthetics
Fatalism ○
◉ Status   ◉ Empathy
○ Appearance   Spenders ○   ○ Creativity   ◉ Infoholic
◉ Convenience   Spiritual ◉   ◉ Esteem   Internationalism ●
Optimism ●   ● Androgyny
◉ Image Awareness
Decor ◉   ● Escapism

● Complexity
Sociability ◉   ● Excitement
Risk ●
Hedonism ●   ● Sexuality

Outer-directed

Inner-directed

● = high attachment

◉ = average attachment

○ = low attachment

© This "Insight '94" Trend Map is copyrighted by Synergy Brand Values Ltd.
Any unauthorised use may be unlawful

26

Grey Generation '94

55 + age group

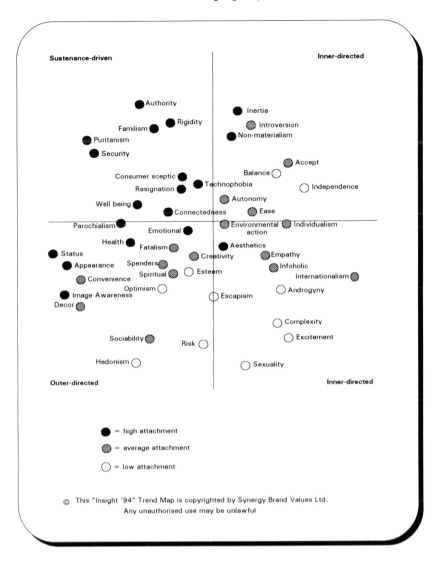

PART THREE:
New tensions and faultlines

We have seen how change has been driven both by aspirations and by necessity. Given the scale of the shifts underway it should be no surprise that the genderquake is rapidly creating new fault lines. Traditional social institutions - family, community and work - are coming under intense strain as rapidly changing values clash with institutions that can adapt only slowly. As always in history, the solution of one set of problems (in this case women's subordination) is creating new ones. In this section we set out some of the starkest problems, and the new lines of tension.

- Women's resentment of slow change

The first set of problems follow on from the value shifts we have already identified. The pace of change seems very rapid to some people, particularly men. But for others, especially women, it appears sluggish, and there is a large gap between official rhetoric and delivery, particularly for those like ethnic minority women who experience 'multiple discrimination'. The facts seem to confirm these concerns: the number of women on the boards of major companies is still negligible at 3.72%[62] and the number of women in top management jobs is still extremely low: 2.8% of senior managers and 9.8%[63] of managers. Women still dominate in low grades and the average woman earner would need a pay rise of almost 40% to match the average male earner;[64] even those women managers who have broken through the glass ceiling would require a pay rise of almost 16% to match the average earnings of a male manager.[65] Women managers still report that their work is less highly valued than men's[66] and that the 'men's club' remains a barrier to their careers.[67] Meanwhile jobs continue to be segregated, albeit in more complex ways. For example in financial services, where women have made major gains in traditionally masculine areas like insurance sales, men are still dominant in the top managerial jobs.[68]

Those looking to institutional champions of change have often been disappointed. There is resentment that whilst initiatives such as Opportunity 2000 have raised awareness of equality issues, they have lacked teeth, whether in terms of criteria for involvement or implementation.[69] The same is true of training: a 'TrainFair' report published last year found that training in equal opportunities in some major companies is still a paper rather than practical commitment.[70]

This mismatch between a culture of high aspirations and institutions that are failing to deliver is causing acute strain. For example, one report found that 43% of women would like help with child care but only 9% of their employers provide it; 49% would like assistance for carers but only 6% of their employers provide it.[71] Women who think they can find equal fulfilment in their work, family and homelife are often left feeling trapped as they juggle too many responsibilities. Significantly, the most educated women in all age groups, who have had the easiest access to the labour market, are the least satisfied both at home and at work: according to one survey 36% of degree educated women are not happy with the demands on their time, over 37% of full time working mothers feel that they have skills at work which are not being applied and 54% that a woman cannot get on at work without support from her family.[72]

Many also feel let down by government. The lack of government action on guaranteeing a public infrastructure of childcare to make it easier for working couples to make varied choices about the balance between work and parenting means that the UK has a higher drop out rate for women with children from the labour market than any other EU country.[73] Synergy data confirms that the optimism of younger women over the age of 25 wanes a little - a product perhaps of encountering obstacles.

There is also an additional irony that women's expectations have peaked at the very time that recession has sharply constrained employers' room for manoeuvre. Economic downturns bring fewer opportunities for promotion, lead some companies to see equal opportunities as an unaffordable luxury, and make male managers even more defensive and resentful of policies that threaten their security.[74]

Targets can exacerbate these tensions. The energetic pursuit of targets for women managers, and schemes for flexitime and maternity leave, often generate equally strong male resentment of what is seen as positive discrimination.[75] As a result some companies like Northern Foods have concentrated instead on the need for more qualitative changes in the attitudes of their workforce.[76] Even in liberal professional organisations there is no shortage of comments like 'If you are a woman and you are black, you're made'.

In this context, it is unsurprising that a survey of women directors two years ago found that 70% thought that women still do not have equal opportunities in the workplace. Male attitudes were cited as the most common problem by 37%. But the same survey found that 90% rejected quotas (currently illegal) in the workplace with 70% also opposing the setting of targets - owing to a fear that they would be accused of not getting a job on their merits.[77]

In traditionally male jobs, where physical strength still remains a factor in employment prospects, the backlash can make everyday work particularly difficult. The experience of women in the London Fire Brigade who benefitted from the positive action strategy devised by the GLC in the 80s is a case in point: without the requisite cultural change many women have found it hard to succeed in a climate of male resentment.[78] In other fields, like the police and army, even fairly modest steps towards equal opportunities have been strongly resisted across the hierarchy.

- Stress and women opting out

Backlashes and uneasy relations between women and men at work are heightening stress amongst many working women. This is particularly true when there are also conflicts with partners over careers, deciding when best to start a family and balancing competing demands at home and at work. Many female managers report feeling that they have to work harder to prove themselves, and that any mistakes are seized upon and blown out of all proportion.[79] Analysts have also repeatedly shown that the pressure to act masculine, confident and aggressive, causes particular stress for women managers, though perhaps less so for a younger generation of more confident, outer-directed and assertive women.

The price of success for women at work can be high: the average female manager is less likely to be married and more likely to be childless than her male counterpart; half of all women managers are childless and they are twice as likely to have been divorced or separated as their male colleagues. The majority of male managers' wives were there to be supportive, whilst the majority of female managers were in a dual earner relationship if they were in one at all.[80] The costs of women's caring role in trying to reconcile career and home is well documented.[81] In the light of these experiences it is no surprise that younger women are emulating the distant role models of successful female managers and are being much more circumspect about when and whether to have children.[82]

Stress is also a big factor leading women managers to opt out of their jobs. Just as there are indications that women are opting out of marriage, so too there are signs that in the workplace a growing number of women are opting out of large organisations. In the USA there is now an extensive literature on women 'bailing out' of employment. Significant subsequent drop-out rates amongst female MBA graduates in the USA suggest that access to equal educational opportunities has not been sufficient to ease women's entry into the best jobs. In one study of MBA graduates a quarter of the female sample were considering leaving their jobs, and most saw organisational environments and cultures as their biggest barrier.

But instead of opting out and back into the home, many women have instead opted to set up their own businesses and employ themselves. The evidence is striking. Women-owned small businesses in the USA have risen from 5% in 1970 to 32% today, with some forecasting that the figure will reach 50% by the year 2000. Between 1982 and 1987 the revenue growth of women owned businesses was four times that of all business. Women in the USA choose self-employment at a rate five times greater than men and are successful in 80% of the businesses they begin. A Gallup poll for the US Department of Labor suggested that almost half of women in the 35-54 age group wanted to start a business, with the figure rising to two-thirds in the 18-34 age group.[83] As a result more Americans are now employed by women-owned businesses than the Fortune 500, contributing to a new business culture of female entrepreneurship.[84]

Much the same seems to be happening in the UK. While one recent report suggested that women's growing presence in management may have been halted[85], the same report also showed that younger women managers (those under 40) are twice as likely to resign as women over 50 and that women in general are twice as likely to resign their positions as men. This phenomenon was described as 'voting with their feet' by the Director of the Institute of Management, Roger Young, who also acknowledged that it was likely that 'some women could be reacting against the non-family-friendly policies of larger companies and are opting to leave behind the stresses of corporation life for the buzz of being in control of their own companies.'

In the UK there are more than 740,000 women running their own businesses - nearly one in four of all self employed people and nearly twice as many in 1980. During 1992/93, 31% of the people setting up their own businesses through the Business Start Up Scheme were women.[86] The extent to which these choices are determined by the desire for a changed lifestyle or by resentment at work remains unclear and merits further research. But one report did find that this desire to be one's own boss was strong amongst all women (31%) and even stronger amongst working mothers at 40%.[87]

This DIY culture of self-promotion is never costless. Running a business brings huge strains on family life, particularly in the early phases. Yet many women are prepared to accept these because of the high value they place on economic independence and control over their own work culture. Perhaps too, the value shift we have identified towards a greater desire for risk is also translating into a vigorous entrepreneurialism.

- Crises in the family

Opting out is clearly becoming a significant phenomenon in work. But in many respects it is a far more visible issue in the family where economic enfranchisement has sharply reduced women's willingness to remain in a subordinate or dependent role in the family. The result has been a steady rise in divorce rates. Britain now has the second highest number of divorces in Europe[88] and is rapidly closing the gap with the USA where half of all marriages end in divorce. The cause is simple. As John Ermisch, an economist from Glasgow University, has shown, right across the world women's financial need for marriage declines as their pay rises relative to men. Those countries with most jobs for women tend to have the highest divorce rates. His study found that mothers who have been employed for four-fifths of the time since the birth of their first child are twice as likely to get divorced as mothers who do not work after child birth.[89]

This shift is occurring across all groups. But its character varies. For example in dual-earner couples - now 60% of the total compared to only 43% in 1973[90] - some of the key tensions come from how parenting and domestic work is shared. The 1991 British Social Attitudes report found that 75% of all women continue to shoulder the main burdens of domestic labour, and in dual-earner families where both men and women work full time, women are still mainly responsible for domestic duties in 67% of households.[91] A more in-depth qualitative study shows that women bear the brunt of the dual earner lifestyle organising child care and domestic responsibilities in all but 10% of the cases.[92]

The Life at 33 report[93] illustrates the gap that exists between attitudes and actual behaviour: 69% of the sample said that men should do the same jobs as women around the house but in practice in 77% of the cases women did the cooking, 66% the shopping, 75% the cleaning and 85% the laundry. This UK data parallels US studies which have found that although women still tend to do fewer hours in employment, once their domestic labour is taken into account they work a full fifteen hours extra unpaid a week, effectively a month's extra work a year.[94] Only time will tell whether younger men who are attached to eliminating gender difference will translate this into behaviour when they become parents.

For now the juggling of responsibilities is leading to unprecedented stress and strains, especially if there are children. Marital satisfaction is particularly low in the period before children go to school, although there are obvious differences between high-income career couples who can afford good quality, home-based child care and blue collar dual-earner families without surplus income. But for all, one of the main causes of stress amongst women is dissatisfaction with their partner's failure to share domestic labour or to accept their need to work.[95]

If dual-earners face difficulties with domestic labour, one of the sharpest tensions for those at the bottom of the scale, is that women whose husbands or partners are unemployed are discouraged from work by the structure of the benefits system; while every other group of women has come to participate more in employment, unqualified women's employment has not increased, primarily because of these disincentives. These 'no-earner' families have become a significant part of British society, and now account for 14.4% of UK households,[96] prone not only to the particular stresses and strains caused by unemployment and poverty, but also to the indirect tensions caused by their male partners' identity crises. Left behind by the bigger shifts in society, there is still a minority of women who are having children early as one way of developing an identity, and who are not following their peers at school into higher aspiration and higher achievement.[97]

- The care deficit

The overall picture is of women's greater autonomy leading them to opt out of those institutions - whether the firm or the family - which no longer meet their needs. As well as divorce and small business creation, this shift is also having dramatic effects elsewhere. In the past, society has depended on the informal role that women play in the family and community - the labour of child care and domestic work, looking after neighbours and providing informal support.

Today, however, as more women go out to work, and as autonomy clashes with the traditional duty to act as carers, a care deficit is emerging. Within the family women's move out of the home has not been matched by men's preparedness to share responsibilities. Within the community, a significant reduction in the availability of informal female care has not been adequately matched either by changes in male behaviour or by formal funded provision to replace the informal work of the past.

These issues are not likely to be easily solved. For example, some have argued for tackling the parenting deficit by encouraging new incentives to stay at home for two years after childbirth. These may be attractive to some, particularly if, as Amitai Etzioni has suggested, they are offered equally to men and women.[98] But our analysis suggests that any policies which sound as if they are prescribing that only women should stay at home are unlikely to resonate with the core values of a considerable portion of the younger generation of women. The same might apply to greater incentives for women to accept the burden of looking after elderly relatives or neighbours. If work and independence become increasingly important to young women, who go on to have fewer children and later in life, and if the population over 85 continues to grow, it is not hard to anticipate stark lines of tension and tough pressures on policy-makers.[99]

- The challenge to male identity

These changes and the new tensions they are bringing are not just a matter of women's rising expectations. They are also being shaped by men's failure or unwillingness to adapt to new roles at work and at home. While a younger generation of men aged between 18-34 are more in tune with the values of women in their age group, it is important not to overstate this convergence. The Synergy data shows that there is still a significant minority, including just under a third of men aged between 18-34, who remain socialised to the dominant male value set and who can be classified as social resisters and survivors - those still clinging on to older identities.

The Henley Centre's data on how people use their time shows how little has changed. Men are spending more time with their children than ten years ago but nothing approaching an equal role in parenting.[100] Instead the majority remain attached to their role as male breadwinner. According to the British Social Attitudes survey nearly half of all fathers agree with the view that 'a husband should be the breadwinner and the wife should look after the home and the children' compared with less than one in four mothers. Fathers were 9% more likely than mothers to believe that 'mothers of pre-schoolchildren should not work outside the home'.[101] Qualitative studies confirm that most men are ambivalent about women working, tending to see it as 'the woman's choice' and downplaying economic pressures to work.[102] Although as we have seen, some men are becoming more amenable to part-time work, many resist it not only for financial reasons but also because they want a reason to escape from parenting responsibilities.[103] In the USA, where the genderquake is more advanced, there is even stronger evidence of men holding onto traditional breadwinner (and even hunter) roles.[104]

In areas of lost manufacturing where young unemployed and unskilled men are joining an older generation in the job queue the insecurity and resentment are predictable. Even men with superficially 'liberal' values sometimes feel that the balance of equality legislation is wrong, seeing positive action as discrimination against 'the white male' and male unemployment as the fault of women.[105]

According to Synergy, compared to young men as a whole, those out of work are more likely to reject their local community, are even more dismissive of traditional sources of authority, more introverted, and more attracted to excitement; a factor which helps to explain their attraction to crime as a way of bolstering their fragile sense of masculinity.[106]

- New forms of discrimination

Some - particularly an older generation of feminists - tend to see male resistance simply as bloody-mindedness. But this ignores the real experience of men - particularly younger ones who have never experienced the confident male superiority of the past. Although much of the backlash is a predictable defence of old privileges, complaints about positive discrimination have a basis in fact. For example, the EOC recently revealed that 40% of complaints about recruitment enquiries were by men claiming job discrimination, with more than half complaining about job segregation. One agency in West Yorkshire is currently under investigation by the EOC for allegedly reserving packing jobs for women.[107] Another small scale survey of employers in the North of England found that men going for 'women's work' were likely to be discriminated against by employers.[108] Job segregation can exacerbate these types of discrimination against men as future job creation is likely to take place mainly in areas where they have been under-represented.

- Male underachievement

If discrimination is an immediate sign of the changing power balance, underlying attitudes, and behaviour in schools, indicate the deep-seated and potentially cumulative nature of change. Synergy's research amongst 15-17 year olds reveals that while girls have become more optimistic boys are becoming pessimistic and introverted. As we have seen, one consequence is that boys are under-performing in schools relative to girls even in so-called 'male' subjects like maths and science, and are failing to make up ground in subjects which used to be seen as more female. Now it is boys who are suffering from low self-esteem, who are less ambitious, less willing to continue in education and more likely than girls to want to start a family. Boys' relative pessimism appears to be affecting their educational performance, setting in motion a vicious spiral as unemployment fuels low aspiration which in turn makes young men unemployable.[109] One extreme symptom is the fact that suicide amongst young men has doubled in the past decade: from 1 in 20,000 of 15-24 year old males in 1979 to 1 in 10,000 in 1989.[110] Policy-makers are only just becoming aware of these new problems, grappling with how to rethink educational policies and equal opportunities strategies to provide targeted measures to improve the performance and confidence of a growing number of young men who are being left behind.

PART FOUR:
Political vehicles for change

We have set out some of the drivers of change - and in particular the value shifts in the seven million generation - and some of the difficult consequences that result as the traditional institutions of marriage, community and work find it hard to keep up with the rate of change. So far we haven't mentioned another set of institutions which should be critical: political parties and movements.

In the past, politics played a central part in the changing relations between men and women not only through the political parties but also through women's organisations, from the feminist campaigns of the mid-19th century, through the suffragettes in the early part of this century to the women's liberation movement of the 1960s and 1970s. Much of the progress that has already been described would never have happened without the legally enshrined political, social and economic rights that they won through bitter struggles.

But in the 1990s, it is striking how much change is taking place well away from the world of politics. As we have seen, employers are now arguably more significant shapers of women's lives than parliaments. Politics is following rather than leading. Whether on gender issues or those concerning young people generally, the new themes and arguments seem to bubble up more from popular culture, lifestyle experimenters and campaigning organisations rather than the political parties and an older generation of women's organisations.

- The gender gap

The changing values of the seven million generation have yet to filter through into a different way of talking about gender and other issues. In the UK gender has yet to materialise as a significant electoral issue, although periodically pollsters acknowledge large gaps in party preferences and issues, and there were particularly big swings amongst women (particularly in social groups C1 and C2) before the 1992 election.[111] Polls tend to show that women generally are more concerned with issues that directly and practically affect the lives of their families and friends - particularly health and education. Not surprisingly, they favour public support for childcare, nursery and after-school activities.[112] But beyond that there is still no distinct women's agenda in mainstream British politics.

Nor has a new generation dispelled older assumptions that women are less political than men. A MORI poll to accompany the 75th anniversary of women's rights[113] showed that 76% of women of all ages were not involved in any form of political activity, and 82% of women aged between 18-24. Four out of ten of these young women said that they had absolutely no interest in politics on the grounds that politics is all talk and no action, that political meetings are boring, that politics is dominated by men and that people only go into politics for themselves.

But it would be wrong to interpret these as implying no pressures and demands. Traditional male dominance over political parties has always made it difficult for them to communicate effectively with women voters, but it is becoming harder for them to be complacent, particularly now that women have become less deferential and a more general climate of antipolitics has taken hold.[114] In other countries, parties have had to take much more active steps than in the UK to change their gender balance and preempt rejection by a more assertive generation of women. For example, Norway's Labour Party decided in the early 1980s that at least 40% (and not more than 60%) of their candidates should be women. The other parties followed, and remarkably quickly gender issues ceased to be controversial (political styles also changed, with noticeably more informality). In Finland, the 1991 election gave 40% of the seats to women, with an average age under 40.[115] In the USA women organised particularly effectively around abortion, and around the Anita Hill case, with big increases in the numbers of governors, senators and representatives in the early 1990s.[116]

In the USA, as in these other countries, women's organisations have proven far better able to translate women's electoral potential into real power. They have highly developed systems of lobbying and influence, numerous research institutes and specialised groups. They have close links with women's media. And they have been able to mobilise ideas and electoral support to shift the parties' policies. Most of this work takes place around Congress and in state legislatures. But it has also had a direct impact on Presidential politics. As well as cultivating a youthful style, Bill Clinton was encouraged to make a direct appeal to working women who rewarded him with a 29% lead over George Bush, easily enough to swing the election.[117]

The lessons to be drawn from these experiences are complex. They seem to suggest that although enforced targets generate resentment (and may alienate a younger generation of women), they do have the potential, as transitional measures, to change the face of political parties. Other countries' experiences also confirm the need to organise effectively, and to raise substantial sums of money to finance professional lobbying and research, and to avoid the kind of duplication which seems to beset the British scene.

- The generation gap

But in politics, as with values more generally, the awakening to gender is inseparable from generational shifts. The rise to prominence of new middle-aged women politicians is coinciding with a far-reaching rejection of politics by young people. In the UK this has manifested itself in many ways.

Youth membership of both the Conservative and Labour party is in historic decline and only one member in 20 in all the main political parties is under the age of 25.[118]

The same detachment is affecting voting. 31% of 18-29 year olds who were eligible to vote in the 1987 General election failed to do so.[119] And as yet unpublished figures suggest that between 43-45% of young people under the age of 25 did not vote in 1992.[120]

This distrust and distance from conventional party politics appears deep-seated. One survey of people in their early thirties found that 39% think politicians are in politics for their own benefit, and 29% that it makes no difference which party is in power.[121] Amongst younger people, especially those below 25, there is even less faith in conventional party politics with many emphasising issues which remain low on the parties' agendas: environmentalism, international campaigns, animal rights and health issues such as AIDS, all seem to excite commitment in a way that traditional politics does not.[122]

Research amongst 16-19 year olds confirms the antipolitics trend. Politicians seem to matter very little to young people. Only 16% rank politicians and parties as an issue of concern. Girls are 10% more likely than boys to be uninterested in party politics and party politicians.[123]

But it would be wrong to conclude that today's young people - whether male or female - are apolitical or unconcerned with the public realm. Many are devoting their energies to voluntary and campaigning organisations which fit their values better and seem able to deliver what they promise. During the 1980s, for example, one of the fastest rises in volunteering took place amongst 18-25 year olds.[124] More than a third of 16-19 year olds felt strongly committed to combatting racism (37%) and sexism (34%) and 26% were concerned about the environment. The problem is rather that, according to the researchers who carried out this survey, 'no existing political party has a set of ideas which fits in with those of the young people studied', particularly 'the issues of concern to young people, such as equal opportunities and the environment.'[125] One effect of this gap is volatility. 80% of those questioned throughout the three year study had changed their voting preferences.[126]

As yet, however, the parties have found no successful ways of channelling these energies and commitments. All three face major problems. The Conservative's apparent nostalgia for an era of fixed, and traditional gender roles, which has been reinforced by the 'back to basics' slogan, does not play well with many younger potential Tory voters who are otherwise attracted to the vision of a meritocratic, enterprise society. The Liberal Democrats start on stronger ground, and are successful with some groups of women, but they too have failed to make much impact on the younger age group, lacking any clear definition. Labour has traditionally had most support amongst 18-24 year olds, but it too is handicapped by a cultural legacy - a labourist, unionist, macho approach which alienates many young voters who have no memory of Labour in power. Although a Blair leadership, youthful and fresh faced, might be expected to enthuse young people, poll data is ambivalent. Soundbites on the dissolution of community and family values may go down well with older voters concerned for their security, but such rhetoric sounds backward looking to young women who are eschewing the family in favour of a career, and to a younger generation of men.

- *The role of the women's movement*

In the past the women's movement, in successive incarnations, has dominated the gender debate. It was one of the key 'new social movements' that developed new themes and ideas that were ignored by the parties. We have already shown some of the evidence of its success. But there are signs that it too may now be unable to push the debate further forward. This is because, like political parties, women's organisations are finding it harder to speak to the concerns of younger women in a language they understand.

Some of the reasons may be internal to the women's movement: for example the rapid absorption of feminists within academia, which has brought with it a heavy weight of jargon and theory, and diverted many of the brightest away from practical engagement and political persuasion. But the more important reason is probably to do with generational experience. The 'post-equality' cohort have never been part of an historic struggle around equality and find the militant language and culture of an earlier generation out of place, as if they have outgrown the movements whose values they have absorbed.

The clearest evidence of this can be found in attitudes to feminism. A 1991 Guardian survey of 1100 women found that only 9% of respondents viewed feminism positively and only 13% belonged to a women's group despite the fact that 51% of those in management positions thought that they were discriminated against and despite the fact that 58% of women thought that there was still discrimination against women in the workplace.[127] Data from the Women's Voices survey in the USA[128] shows a similar pattern on the other side of the Atlantic.

Amongst younger women this distancing is even more striking. 75% of women in a Cosmopolitan survey of female students in the UK said that they were ambitious whilst only 38% described themselves as feminist.[129] Other studies show that young women preface their belief in equal rights for women with a disclaimer about feminism itself.[130] In a recent survey of women (and men) students in a number of Scottish universities only a minority identified with feminists and more than half made negative comments about them.[131]

An older generation tends to blame these results on a male-dominated media which has stereotyped and demonised feminists as demonic man-haters. There is certainly a problem with their media image. But the women's movement in the UK, as in the USA, must also bear some responsibility for failing to attract the next generation. Its antagonism to femininity has clearly alienated many, as has its strident tone, dogmatism and sectarianism. The increased emphasis upon the enjoyment of sexuality, a trend identified by Synergy amongst 15-17 year olds, highlights this dilemma for women's organisations seeking to appeal to young women.[132]

The failure to win a new generation also reflects the failure to develop new messages that go beyond the assertion of rights relative to men and the demand for quantitative changes. These arguments antagonise a younger generation of women who value the blurring of gender difference and who find the demanding language and message of the movement alienating. Given that there are bigger differences in values between older and younger women than between younger women and younger men, we should probably not be surprised.

- The backlash

The extent to which women (especially younger women) have become part of a 'backlash' against feminism has been written about widely by authors like Susan Faludi and Marilyn French.[133] Male authors have also pushed the issue up the agenda, some acting as spokesmen for the 'men's rights movement'. Michael Crichton's book *Disclosure* centres around a powerful female executive who makes a pass at a male colleague and on rejection proceeds to accuse him of sexually harassing her.[134] Pro-feminist men like Warren Farrell, the only man to have been elected three times on the New York council of the National Organisation for Women, argue that the equality agenda has now become the 'inequality' agenda.[135]

Similar views are gaining ground in the UK with authors like David Thomas and Neil Lyndon[136] publicising the prevalence of male victims of domestic violence or sexual harassment of men by women, with an ever zealous media quick to jump on the latest 'post-feminist' bandwagon. There are also signs of change at the grass roots. The strength of the men's rights lobby mobilising against the Child Support Agency is a case in point - witness the televisual images of divorced men thronging the streets of London, second wives and children in tow, and the demonising of Ros Hepplewhite, its former Chief Executive, as a strident feminist, a divorcee hell-bent on wreaking revenge on all absent fathers. Controversies around date rape and sexual harassment by women are also gaining currency. And this year an International Men's day was even proclaimed in blatant competition to International Women's Day.

One overriding theme is dominant: the fear that the gender issue has now come full circle with men the new victims, discriminated against by a legislative framework of equal opportunities, and a climate of political correctness which skews power too much in the direction of women and an economic climate which needs their skills.

Feminists have argued - less so here in the UK it is worth noting - that evidence of resentments, managerial resistance and heightened gender tension in the workplace, even the growth of an anti-feminist 'men's rights' movement, is something to be expected - that men could never be expected to relinquish power gracefully and that they are simply shouting in the transitional phase of a power shift.

But as we have already seen, this response now looks increasingly inadequate, both as analysis and as strategy. The women's movement's responses to the signs of a political backlash have shown a lack of political maturity. By downplaying issues such as male sexual harassment or discrimination,[137] rather than putting them in context, they lose credibility and the ability to forge wider coalitions. They give the appearance of holding onto a bulldozer radicalism that exacerbates tensions, and actually impedes change.

Moreover they demonstrate that their analysis - which denies the possibility that women may abuse power - is now too narrow for the times. Although there is nothing resembling parity in terms of abuse - there is now no shortage of evidence of sexual abuse by women of children, of male victims of domestic violence,[138] and of women sexually harassing male colleagues. Women are clearly able to abuse power when they have it. If anything the value shifts amongst a younger generation of women - their outer-directedness and increasing 'maleness' - seem likely to translate into an enjoyment of power and a rise in phenomena such as sexual harassment of men. These arguments are unpalatable for a strand of feminist thinking which errs towards arguing about the 'essential qualities' of femaleness, and assumes that a world ruled by women would not abuse power in the same way that men have. But issues of this kind are inevitably going to rise to prominence as power shifts.

There is a further, perhaps even more fundamental, problem for the women's movement. The very identity of the movement is predicated on the need for a separate agenda for women. This has inevitably made it hard to coopt sympathetic younger men. But in the post-equality generation the convergence between men's attitudes and women's cannot be ignored. Young men and women have increasingly similar attitudes not only to work and politics but even to feminism itself.[139] Simply in terms of political tactics this suggests that women's issues should no longer be seen in isolation.

Some 'women's organisations' have begun to recognise the need to address how the equality culture is affecting men: the Working Mothers Association's change of name to Parents At Work is one such example, a response to the growing number of calls they received from men about the problems of being a working parent. Significantly, however, the change was criticised from the conventional feminist stance.[140]

PART FIVE:
New Agendas

- An historic shift

The evidence set out in this paper reveals a complex series of value shifts: a long-term rise in the importance of autonomy, and a shift in power towards women and in values towards more feminine and inner-directed ones. These are symptoms of an historic transformation in the roles of men and women. This shift, which may also involve a shift away from the 200 year separation of home and work,[141] is having many effects ranging from unemployment to crime. It is so fundamental that we should not be surprised that many find it hard to acknowledge, let alone to cope.

The combination of changing attitudes and changing economic needs gives us strong grounds for believing that there really is 'no turning back'; no serious prospect of a return to the institutions and values of the past. Some forecast that ageing societies will return to traditional values. On the basis of past evidence, our guess is that when ageing becomes a really serious policy issue in the early years of the next century, the values of today's 18-34 year olds, who will then be in middle- and old age, and dominating social values, will not have changed substantially. Like a minority of today's 50-somethings, who are spending much more on travel and leisure, they will still value autonomy, experimentation and the chance to realise themselves. And, just as today, they will resist attempts to force them into preconceived roles.

In the meantime however it is the gap between dominant institutions and the seven million generation's values that is the problem. Whether in business, politics or the public sector those institutions which want to thrive through the early decades of the next century will need to adapt both in terms of what they do and how they do it.

Surprisingly, perhaps, the lessons for parties, employers and even women's organisations are not that dissimilar. To appeal to this generation they need to reflect their styles and values. For those who become involved, they need to offer variety and feedback. If they want respect as organisations they need to be focused in their goals and achievements, with clear links between inputs and outputs, promising less and delivering more. In their language, they need to be more at ease with the complexity and ambiguity that is such a feature of the age, and to address people as individuals, not as members of groups. They need to be visibly diverse, and at home with gender equity. They need to respect the desire for autonomy in all areas of life, and to respond to the aspiration for more varied and balanced lives. And they need to take seriously the growing commitments to the environment and internationalism.

- Seven new themes

But these are only starting points. A successful transition to new models of work, parenting and leisure will demand radical rethinking across many different policy areas. The following section sets out a far from comprehensive list of seven new themes which should be the starting point for any institutions concerned with gaining power and legitimacy in the decades ahead.

i) Expanded Rights

Our inherited framework of rights has become outmoded. It was designed for an era when men worked fulltime and women stayed at home. It now needs to be extended to fit the new working, living and learning realities of our times. That means providing new frameworks to guarantee pensions, benefits and learning opportunities for the growing number of women (and men) whose work is discontinuous, part-time and insecure. It means devising new ways of coping with the impact of discontinuous work on the private costs of mortgages, pensions and private healthcare. It means offering men parallel rights to women in terms of paternity leave and childcare, to symbolise a more balanced distribution of responsibilities. And it requires new rights to the things which are needed to make opportunities real: above all access to the time and skills which are needed for fulfilled, balanced and successful lives.

ii) The link to responsibilities

But rights alone are not enough. An evolution is taking place in the terms of the political argument. The shift to inner-directedness is bringing a greater stress on personal responsibility as the corollary of autonomy. People want to be able to make choices - but they are also more prepared to carry the consequences of those choices. This new ethos may offer some hope: the potential for new frameworks which link rights and responsibilities. For example, new freedoms to control reproduction and enjoy diverse forms of family can be linked to clearer responsibilities for both men and women to provide financial support to children. Rights to childcare - again for both men and women - can be linked to responsibilities to play an active role in childcare centres or schools.[142] Rights to continuing education can be linked to clearer responsibilities on those who achieve high incomes to pay back the costs.

iii) Infrastructures of support

Real choice, and the ability to act responsibly, often rests on infrastructures of support. The absence of these means that womens' attempts to realise careers and families are causing huge stresses. To relieve these, the whole institutional structures of support need to change. Some of these concern simple things, like changing school hours (or rather guaranteeing activities in the late afternoon and evening) to fit the realities of dual-earner parents and to enable single parents to work. Public institutions (like GP's surgeries) could do far more to fit their times of opening to the needs of families where the parent or parents work.

Other obvious examples are childcare support and continuing education. In both cases women, and increasingly men, look both to government and to employers.

There are options which could benefit all parties without incurring additional costs: for example turning women's and men's national insurance contributions into an account to be drawn down for training sabbaticals or periods of parenting; extending tax relief for workplace and personal childcare; further raising allowances for low income women to purchase childcare.

Employers could seek to cultivate more balanced working environments with less emphasis on long hours and more on quality of output, more imaginative support services to help with crises at home, better conceived policies for flexibility for women (and men) to move in and out of work, and greater encouragement for homework. In each of these cases policies need to become more gender-neutral.

Meanwhile, society as a whole could help reinvigorate the role of the extended family and other community networks; taking advantage of declining mobility and ageing to bring grandparents more fully into parenting, and, where there are no grandparents in the vicinity, organising mentoring or guardian relationships to help parents cope.[143]

iv) *Targeting new areas of disadvantage*

Disadvantage changes its nature over time. Some of the most disadvantaged today are single women - particularly the lone mothers whose participation in work has declined in recent years. They need a raft of new supports such as the low income allowance for childcare, reformed benefits structures to make it easier to work part-time and training to match that available to women going to university. These policies could also help single male parents. But there are also other groups becoming disadvantaged, particularly a minority of unskilled young men. Helping them may require a raft of different types of policy: action to provide activities (or community service) during school holidays or instead of unemployment; long-term subsidies for job creation for younger males to reverse the cycle of low aspirations amongst boys; special training schemes to encourage men to apply for jobs in service industries; mentoring networks linking younger and older men; marketing campaigns to change the identity of jobs; and incentives for men to share in parenting. All of these will be essential not only for the men themselves but also to reduce the indirect pressure their problems impose on to women. Properly conceived they offer the ideal for any government: potentially self-financing policies that reduce the extent to which the interactions of men and women are a zero-sum game.

v) *Revaluing care*

Women's subordinate economic position has much to do with how we value care. Women dominate in both paid and unpaid caring roles, which have tended to be undervalued. Today, in part because of women's enfranchisement, we face a crisis of care. If women continue to go out to work, and men do not take up or are not enabled to pursue their parenting responsibilities, and care for elderly relatives, the care deficit will worse. One effect will be to exacerbate the pressures on working women, who continue to feel a duty to care, but resent the assumption that they should have to bear its full burden. Another will be to throw greater responsibilities on to the state.

If this crisis of care is to be resolved big changes will be necessary. One will be to find ways to replace informal care with more formal, and paid for care. This will be very costly, and will divert resources from other areas of spending. A second will be to encourage more men into caring roles, through reshaping their image and active promotion of a less segregated labour market. A third will be to devise new caring relationships, both within and outside the family, organised through voluntary organisations working in conjunction with professionals. A fourth will be to socialise young people, particularly men, into the world of caring work through community service before entering the labour market or going on to higher education.[144]

vi) From equality to diversity

Big employers are increasingly shifting away from the language of equal opportunities to the language of diversity. They realise that they can get the best out of their employees if they provide structures that give all of them opportunities to contribute.[145] Service companies in particular can best succeed in the market if they reflect the makeup of their consumers, particularly with their front-line staff.

Those that go down this route may find a better fit with the values of the seven million generation. Many younger women find the current approach in equal opportunities problematic. They are ill at ease with targets and any policies which treat them as a distinct group. This may reflect a subliminal absorption of backlash arguments. But it may also reflect their belief that gender roles are becoming blurred.

We now need a much richer notion of equal opportunities that combines rights with a sense of culture. Cultural change has become a priority in many organisations. It can rarely be achieved only by the bulldozer of quantitative targets. Instead these need to become more sophisticated and matched by initiatives that head off resentments and encourage individual employees to own change. Measures to accommodate resistant men need to be combined with highly visible changes in behaviour by top management, champions and mentors. The same applies in government and in politics. Our goal should be to make all institutions better reflect the gender, ethnic and age makeup of the population.

vii) Policies for home as well as work

A happy transition to new patterns of working will depend as much on equality at home as at work. Scandinavian countries, particularly Sweden, have had generous schemes of paternity leave for men as well as women, and schemes to pay the carer to remain at home for the early years of a child's life: both signs of a willingness to recognise the value of home life and parenting. Take up of parenting benefits by men is now rising from a low base. In Scandinavia as a whole one effect is that there is less material inequality between men and women than elsewhere in Europe (although the labour market remains one of the most segregated by gender). Their acute problem, however, is that they now appear to be unable to maintain the generous welfare system which underpins this.[146] When there are downwards pressures on welfare spending it is vital that schemes of this kind are not the first to go.

Linking all of these schemes together will be the job of new styles of leadership.[147] Achieving these transitions will demand a lot of leaders. Each step will be uncertain: in some respects a step into the unknown, culturally, socially and economically. To help in the transition, leaders need to absorb the leading edge values that we have identified. Instead of offering patriarchal leadership from the top they too need to become at ease, able to achieve balance and to cope with complexity. They need to steer away from old styles - pretending that they know all the answers - and instead be seen to learn with their employees and supporters about changes which will never be straightforward.

Conclusion: no turning back

The two great shifts identified in this paper, the genderquake which is passing power to women and the generational changes in values, are profound and irreversible. There really is no turning back from the new attachments to autonomy. And there are no institutions or leaders with the legitimacy to return our society to older values and older roles.

But there is much to play for and much that can go wrong. Many women in the seven million generation are set to opt-out, not only from marriage and childbirth, but also from working for large resistant organisations. For many the results are greater independence. But opting out can also exacerbate the tensions: the gaps that divide the mainstream from the leading edge and the mutual resentments in society, workplaces and families that are already growing.

That is why it is so important for leaders to take heed. They should not expect the pendulum to swing back. The changes in values, particularly women's values, are deep-seated and cumulative and, barring unexpected events like wars or catastrophes, they are likely to continue. Those leaders who choose to swim against the tide of change may win short-term gains, appealing to all those who feel disoriented by the loss of familiar landmarks. But in time this strategy will render them marginal. By contrast, the party which can develop a political language and agenda which resonates with the core values of the seven million generation will benefit enormously in future general elections.

For decision-makers the priority now is to understand not to resist. Whether as voters, consumers, employees or trade union members the seven million generation will before too long be in the driving seat. They already make up nearly a third of the electorate and are becoming increasingly volatile. The seven million women in particular will be far more assertive than previous generations. Over the medium term institutions have a simple choice: they can either rethink their values and adapt to change or be rendered irrelevant by it.

Summary

There are seven million women and over seven million men in the UK between the ages of 18 and 34. They are the **first post-equality generation**, brought up after the achievement of equal opportunities legislation and a culture that has turned against discrimination. They are now having to resolve complex choices without clear precedents: balancing work and home, coping with more fluid identities. But **opinion leaders remain largely ignorant** of their values and concerns.

Evidence of values and atittudes suggests **major generational differences**, particularly amongst women. Younger women value autonomy, work and education more than family or parenting. In addition to culture and technology a key **driver of change is economics**: the large shift of women into work; the feminisation of the economy and jobs; companies becoming more aware of the need to develop policies that attract and retain women. This is being pushed further by women's greater success in education, itself in part a response to the changing labour market.

Some **men are adapting** to the changing balance between men and women in the economy. They are coming to terms with parenting roles; applying for what used to be 'women's jobs'; forming 'men's groups' on council estates. There is evidence of a convergence of younger men's and women's values. But **many men are failing to adapt**. Domestic labour is still very unequally shared. Most men still expect to be breadwinners. Others are reacting badly against their declining status and pay, particularly at the bottom of the labour market.

The result is a **new set of fissures**. Tension is rising in the home with more divorce, one consequence of womens greater economic independence. Many women are resentful of the slow pace of change within firms. There are signs of stress, particularly amongst high achievers, and significant numbers of women are opting out. Men are beginning to complain about **discrimination**, particularly in services. There is also a broader cultural backlash against the equality agenda on both sides of the Atlantic.

Both **women's organisations and political parties are failing** to be adequate vehicles for change, partly because of value gaps between them and the younger generation.

But **a new agenda is slowly emerging**, for employers as well as political organisations. It involves new styles and a new culture. It is concerned about new forms of flexible work, about new rights, autonomy and responsibility, about finding ways to persuade men to embrace equality, and about revaluing the roles of parenting and caring.

Evidence suggests that **the value shifts are deeply rooted** and are unlikely to be reversed by a more socially conservative 'family values' or 'back to basics' agenda. Instead those institutions which are seen to embrace the emerging values are likely to do best in winning the commitments of the 18-34 age group, whether as consumers, employees or voters.

Appendix - Explaining the Value Maps;

(i) About Synergy Brand Values Ltd:

Synergy Brand Values Ltd is a consultancy which helps clients understand peoples' underlying values, beliefs and motivations and how they are likely to change. It analyses the impact of dynamic social and cultural change on market structures. The majority of their work is done with commercial firms - helping them to identify consumer values which affect their markets so as to develop effective corporate and branding strategies. Synergy's developmental model is based on the premise, confirmed by a large body of evidence, that people's values, beliefs and motivations are relatively consistent and change only slowly. These values and motivations influence attitudes and lifestyles which in turn influence behaviour.

In this paper, data has been analysed by Helen Wilkinson of Demos and Pat Dade of Synergy Brand Values Ltd to provide an historical tracking of how values have changed, in particular showing how the values of particular age groups differ from previous generations when they were the same age.

(ii) About the survey:

The sample size

The value map data comes from the Insight '94 Survey carried out by Synergy Brand Values Ltd. A random sample of 2,500 15-75 year old adults were interviewed throughout the UK during October 1993. The questionnaire was split into an interviewer administered part - covering basic demographic data including media consumption and attitudes - and a self administered part covering questions which probe the deep seated values, beliefs and motivations of the respondents.

The methodology

The analysis is based on a typology of values which is used to classify people according to their value structure. The British typology was developed in 1978/79 based on a longitudinal survey begun in 1973. It drew on two methodologies:

• the analysis of social type values pioneered by Dr Arnold Mitchell of the Stanford Research Institute in the USA;

• a set of methods for understanding societal trends similar to those of the Yankelovich monitor in the USA. The combined model was developed by Taylor Nelson, now Taylor Nelson/AGB and subsequently licensed to Synergy Brand Values Ltd.

Copyright of this material rests with Synergy Brand Values. Demos is grateful to Synergy for permission to analyse, interpret and publish their data for this project - the first time this has been made publicly available. Interpretation and the context in which it is used are the responsibility of the author alone.

(iii) The significance of the positioning of the value clusters:

People's values are plotted on a map by use of Principle Components Analysis. By merging this map of values with its developmental model, Synergy is able to track the way the UK's society's values are changing and the importance of the value changes underway. Over recent decades values clusters have tended to move in a clockwise direction around the map on the page opposite. The clustering methodology used means that the centre of the map reflects the core values of the British population. The map overleaf shows the three main stages of development which individuals, and society as a whole, have gone through:

• **Sustenance-driven values:** the values which are in the main in the top left hand side of the map used to be dominant. They contributed to the political consensus in favour of the welfare state. They are concerned predominantly with security: physical, economic and moral sources of authority. In this value set the traditional family and community are central.

The rise of the welfare state and economic growth meant that most of these traditional sustenance driven values were satisfied for a majority of the British population. As a result these values have become less central and are gradually becoming less significant. Currently, classes C2 and DE cluster here the most. The generational effect is obvious - they are held most strongly by the 55+ generation and most weakly by those under 34, especially those under 25.

• **Outer-directed values:** over time, *traditional* values have been pushed away from the centre by the cluster of 'outer-directed' values on the bottom left hand side. These values have been gradually rising in importance since 1945: they became central to the British value map in the late 70s with the

British Values '94

all ages

62

breakdown of the post-war consensus around the welfare state and a growing individualism. These values emphasise status, image and consumerism. Politically they help us to understand the appeal of Thatcherism, and its ability to transcend older class boundaries. In the 1990s however they have become less central as a new set of values have pushed through.

• **Inner-directed:** the values on the top and bottom right hand side of the map are the leading edge values, signposting the likely direction of change. The values on the bottom right hand side of the map are the strongest leading edge values - some of which are gradually moving towards the centre and becoming core values. These values represent a deepening of feminisation (that is the wider acceptance of values which have traditionally been seen as female) and can be characterised as inner-directed: they include non-materialism, acceptance, ease, empathy, complexity and androgyny. They are held most strongly by the 18-34 generation, especially the under 25s, very little by those over 55+. The values on the top right hand side are even more fringe than the values on the bottom right hand side. They are only held by a small percentage of the British population, predominantly inner-directed people from classes AB, and by young people.

• **The current British value map:**

The values which cluster at the centre of the map are core to the current British value system. The map confirms the move from outer-directed to more inner-directed values. Synergy's long term 'tracking' of values suggests that infoholics, androgyny, escapism, risk, complexity and excitement are the leading edge values which we can expect to move into the centre and become the core values in the future.

(iv) Patterns of adherence

These value maps can be analyzed to probe differences across a range of criteria - gender, age and class. We have developed a coding system which allows us to see how a particular sub-group differs from the base average of the UK population as a whole. The grey colour tone indicates an average attachment to that particular value. It is the benchmark on which attachments to particular clusters of values can be assessed. Black indicates an above average attachment to a particular value or cluster, and white a below average attachment, in other words a rejection of a particular value or cluster. (In both cases this is on the basis of a 90% confidence level).

When analysing sub-groups within an age group, it is important to remember the relationship of this age group's values to the average and to other generations.

(v) The meaning of the value labels
(in alphabetical order)

Synergy have identified a trend index by structuring certain questions to probe allegiance to a particular concept or value. The following section explains the meaning of the various value labels, some of which are more complex than their labels may imply.

• *Aesthetics:* People who value aesthetics believe that beautiful, unique and different things can be valued in their own right and do not need to justify their existence through their utility.

• *Androgyny:* People who value androgyny see a blurring between feminine and masculine roles. They would argue that there should be no fixed roles for men and women and that women and men are equal. They also subscribe to the view that certain qualities like gentleness, sensitivity, independence and strength, are not the preserves of one sex or another and believe that it would not be a problem if they were born a member of the opposite sex.

• *Acceptance:* These are the 'wise' people: they know of the limits and barriers which individuals face to achieving what they want and accept that these exist. Such people tend to believe that individuals are not entirely responsible for much of what goes on in the world, that even if you know what you want, getting what you want is not easy and that as a result it is important to live your life the way that is best for you. They would also tend to believe that winning in a competitive situation is not as important as taking part.

• *Appearance:* People who value appearance do so not just for their own self esteem but also for approval from others. They believe that spending time on their appearance is important.

• *Authority:* People who remain attached to authority tend to be deferential, hold a strong belief in moral codes and 'traditional' sources of legitimacy - whether in politics, religion, or the family. They tend to see life in very black and white terms - for example, they believe that rules should always be obeyed and never bent and that honesty is important at all times and lying is never an excuse. People who value 'authority' in this sense tend to be older (especially 55+), more backward looking and nostalgic for an era of fixed certainties (values such as androgyny are not on their value map at all). Women's attachment to authority (whilst rejecting other values in the sustenance driven section) can be explained through their role as primary carer and the need to instil a sense of right and wrong with their children)

• *Autonomy:* People who value their autonomy tend to believe that being an individual rather than a member of the crowd is important, and that self-satisfaction rather than approval from others is most important. They like to learn how to do things in their own right and, when making plans, they think of their own needs first before others.

• *Balance:* People valuing balance tend to believe that drive and ambition are not crucial to success. They are not overly concerned with proving to themselves that they can do something; they avoid overworking on one particular aspect of their life - whether sport or work - and are at ease with what they do.

• *Connectedness:* This is something of a New Age value. People who are up on this value tend to believe that individuals are integral to a larger project; that they are part of a universal spirit; that the universe is an interrelated system to which individuals are crucial, and that every individual action, no matter how small, has wider repercussions.

• *Consumer-sceptic*: People high on this value tend to believe that manufacturers could make better products if they had the will and that as a result the public need a 'consumer watchdog' to protect their interests. Consumer-sceptics are people who feel that few products live up to the image of the advertisers and they subscribe to the notion that products these days do not last as long as they used to and that manufacturers spend too much time on presentation and packaging.

• *Convenience:* People high on this value believe that there is never enough time in the day to do what is necessary and that as a consequence 24 hour services are crucial for convenience and for people to fit things into a time that suits them best.

• *Creativity:* Creative people do not necessarily see themselves as artistic nor are they necessarily artistic. However, they enjoy making things themselves, whether making and giving presents or arts and crafts.

• *Complexity:* People who value complexity think it is important to be able to see the possibilities in a situation rather than adjusting to facts as they are. Such people tend to take on more than they can handle, enjoy thinking about things which cannot be proved, and are better at dealing with unexpected situations than following carefully structured and well thought out plans.

• **Decor conscious:** People who are decor conscious tend to be outer-directed and status driven. They spend time improving the appearance of their home and enjoy keeping up with current trends in home decoration. They frequently have lots of possessions and choose possessions which will go with the rest of the room.

• **Ease:** A person at ease is someone who doesn't get nervous easily, who doesn't worry about small things, or about what may happen in the near future; nor do they worry about going out alone at night and feel safe in the area they live.

• **Emotional:** Emotional people would get embarrassed by people making scenes in public, but at the same time feel emotional with strong music, are strongly affected by emotional situations and have often felt like crying for a friend.

• **Empathy:** Empathetic people find it easy to understand how things upset other people; try to understand other people's feelings whatever the situation; understand other people's problems and frequently become their friends' confidantes.

• **Environmental Action:** People high on this value do not believe that we can rely on technology to solve environmental problems and that we need to take more care of the environment if we are to survive. They would stop buying products from companies which cause damage to the environment.

• **Esteem:** These people tend to see things generally working out the way they want them to. They feel successful and useful.

• **Escapist:** Escapist people are open to seeing things which are not necessarily really there; enjoy being able to escape into a world of make believe; they want something but do not know what it is; sometimes feel that they and the world around them is not real and sometimes find it hard to tell where daydreams and reality begin.

• **Excitement:** People who want excitement enjoy doing things which other people consider dangerous. They like violent weather such as storms, thunder and lightning, high winds. They don't believe that risk taking is necessarily selfish and irresponsible.

• *Familism:* People high on 'familism' tend to be attached to other 'traditional' values. They value close family ties, enjoy feeling tied down and like spending their free time at home. They believe in the centrality of the traditional patriarchal family and those most attached to this value are 55+. Women who are still attached to this value whilst rejecting other 'traditional' values still value the enjoyment in their life that comes from the family.

• *Fatalism:* Fatalistic people feel that things, even tragedies and disasters happen for a reason. They believe that things which happen to them were meant to happen.

• *Health:* People who value health see it as a way of life and not something which you are born with. They believe that healthy people make an effort to be full of vitality and energy. They are prepared to give up certain foods in order to be healthy and exercise regularly.

• *Hedonism:* Hedonistic people believe that the pursuit of pleasure is what life is about. They enjoy giving themselves treats, seek pleasure from their own bodies (for example through sports) and want as much pleasure as possible.

• *Individualism:* Individualistic people do not believe that it is necessary to say things to people which they will necessarily like in order to get on with them. They do not always go along with what people want; are not concerned about approval of their way of life either from their family or neighbours.

• *Inertia:* People trapped in inertia are not self aware - they don't know their good or their bad points - and therefore do not work on them. They don't believe it is important.

• *Infoholic:* Infoholics are people who read anything and everything that comes their way and are excited by new ideas in science and technology. They also find what many people might perceive to be useless or irrelevant information interesting.

• *Introversion:* Introverted people are quiet and reserved; hard to get to know; tend to talk easily only when they know people and to talk to one person at a time within a group.

• *Independence:* Independent people of both genders tend to think that people can be complete as individuals without needing a partner to love. They also believe that time spent with a partner whom they love is not vital.

• *Internationalism:* Internationalists do not think it is important to buy British; nor are they necessarily proud of being British. They do not accept the idea that there are too many foreigners in Britain and they don't take great pride in British history and its traditions.

• *Image Awareness:* People who are aware of their image tend to think that it is better to work out their own values and beliefs; they seek to stand out in a group through their dress sense or the way they talk and they choose products which match their personality.

• *Non-Materialism:* Non-materialistic people are not always thinking of what to buy next; they happily do without many things and do not consider it important to earn and spend money. Their philosophy is 'less is more'.

• *Optimism:* Optimists think that life is fun and that even with life's ups and downs, they are confident that everything will turn out fine. They feel good about what the future holds and approach things with energy and enthusiasm.

• *Parochialism:* Parochial people identify strongly with the people living in their area; they are prepared to spend their time helping the local community and like to keep up with local events and local news. They also have a large group of friends and neighbours they can turn to.

• *Puritanism:* Puritanical people tend to believe in the sanctity of heterosexuality and that individuals should work hard, be moral, stay out of trouble, and be punished if they transgress. The same people tend to think that people who dislike hard work also have weak characters. Such people also tend to believe that strict discipline is in a child's best interests; and that criminals should be punished with maximum prison sentences to make them learn their lesson;

• *Resignation:* Resigned people tend to believe that there is no point in trying because it will not make any difference; people who have little hope in life; they are not excited about life; they often feel at their best when they have nothing to do and spend a lot of time doing nothing.

• *Rigidity:* Such people tend to value the traditional way of doing things and rely on a well defined set of rules in their approach to life. People who value rigidity tend to have fixed views, believing that the tried and tested way is the best; and that people should have clear cut rules to live by, they tend to rely on rationality rather than emotion when making decisions.

• **Risk:** People who enjoy risk are often gamblers by nature; prepared to take a risk to make money; willing to start up a business on their own and enjoy playing the Stock Exchange because it is risky.

• **Security:** People for whom security is important believe in saving a little each month even if it means depriving themselves of something. They are people with something put aside to cope with an unexpected expense and who know exactly where they are with their expenses.

• **Sexuality:** People high on sexuality think that sex is important. They take great pleasure in it, are not prescriptive about sexual habits and are willing to experiment.

• **Sociability:** Sociable people show their feelings freely; enjoy making new friends; make an effort to be amusing and go out and see a lot of people.

• **Spenders:** People high on this value are not interested in being careful with money. They are the sorts of people who would respond to a sudden windfall by spending without thinking, who frequently spend more than they intend in shops, who go to sales to look for bargains, often buy the cheap brand and know which shops have the best prices. They are conspicuous consumers to a great extent.

• **Spirituality:** People for whom spirituality is important are often not religious in the conventional sense. Spiritual people are those who believe that individuals have identities which live on after their death; that people can channel energy from the spiritual world; people who have had a mystical or spiritual experience and believe that people are part of a world consciousness or spirit.

• **Status:** Status oriented people believe that achieving a better position in life is worth putting effort into; they believe that job titles and grades at work are important to show individual success compared to others; where one buys a product is as important as the product itself; they are also people who want to be looked up to and respected and who like to live in the 'right area'.

• *Technophobia:* Technophobes are people who believe that technology causes more problems than it solves; who value old order technologies like dials rather than touch buttons on appliances; who find science and technology remote and incomprehensible and who find programmable equipment scary. Typically they would underuse the functions of equipment at home.

• *Well Being:* These people tend to believe that being healthy is an attitude of mind; that people tend to be either naturally healthy or not, and that there is little one can do about it; that you can't really be fit and full of life if you aren't happy in yourself.

Footnotes

1. Source: OPCS figures for 1992 (the most up to date OPCS figures). To be precise there are 7,423,335 women and 7,707,706 men between the ages of 18-34.

2. Despite constituting over a quarter of the UK population, only 2% of MPs in Parliament are under 34 . Source: % calculated from information supplied by the House of Commons Public Information office. The figure is correct as of 30 September 1994.

3. Their work parallels similar work carried out around the world by Professor Ronald Inglehart and his colleagues in the World Values Group.

4. Synergy's data shows that even unemployed women are broadly in tune with the value map illustrated. The only women who are the exception are those women who choose not to work. They are also not particularly positive about full time motherhood, (even if they have children) and tend to feel tied down by the family. They are also more resigned, pessimistic, and have less self esteem.

5. Superwoman Keeps Going: Understanding the Female Web. A survey of women's lives and expectations. National Council of Women of Great Britain, 1992, p 8-9.

6. The following soap characters illustrate this: Beth in Neighbours and a whole range of characters in Brookside such as Mandy Jordache who has not been called to account for the murder of her husband; Beth, her daughter who has come out as a lesbian; her sister Rachel, the pioneer on the local football team; and the role reversal in parenting/career terms between the young successful black career woman, Marianne and her partner, Mick.

7. British Broadcasting Council: Research Working Paper IX: Perspectives of Women on Television, May 1994

8. Paul Gregg, Jobs and Justice: Why Job Creation Alone Will Not Solve Unemployment. Work and Welfare: Tacking the Jobs Deficit, Commission on Social Justice, IPPR, 1993, p32. Stephen Machin and Jane Waldfogel, The Decline of the Male Breadwinner, LSE Welfare State Programme, WSP/103, 1994.

9. Viewpoint, A Changing Workforce, Incomes Data Services, Report 640, May 1993, p.1.

10. Some people have claimed that women will overtake men in employment in 1994/5. However the evidence suggests that this claim may be exaggerated.

11. Paul Gregg, Jobs and Justice: Why Job Creation Will Not Solve Unemployment. Work and Welfare: Tackling the Jobs Deficit, Commission on Social Justice, IPPR, 1993, p41.

12. Fiscal Studies, Institute of Fiscal Studies, Volume 14, No 4, November 1993, p32 Table 14

13. These percentages have been worked out from figures published in Social Trends 1994, HMSO/CSO, Table 4.12, p59.

14. For further information about US trends see: Working Women: More Time for New Approaches by Linda Tarr-Whelan, Centre for Policy Alternatives, Washington DC.

15. Source: Annual Statistical Report, 1993, Law Society (England and Wales). They report a rising trend of women registering for solicitors articles. 1985/86 (earliest figures available) - 45% women. 1992/93 - 54.4% female. An 8.6% increase in the last seven years. They are 'optimistic' that this trend will continue. Source: Institute of Chartered Accountants (England & Wales). In accountancy the proportion of women in the 82/3 intake was 26.6%, of 92/93

intake - 37.1%, a 10.5% increase in a decade. There is also a cohort effect as more women are choosing 'male' subjects at University, and will then go on to increase the numbers in the labour force in years to come.

16. Review of Economy and Employment, Occupational Studies, Managerial, Professional and Technical Occupations, Institute of Employment Research, University of Warwick, 1993

17. In just under 70% of car sales, women either take the decision or have an equal say. This has led to changes in car advertising and front line staffing in garages. Glenda Cooper, Women in the Driving Seat, The Independent, 1994.

18. Advertising is imbued with images which emphasise women's autonomy and independence and the importance of a car to do this. The advertisement celebrating 'getting divorced' rather than getting married is one such example and many reiterate the central message that the car is needed as a source of independence and freedom at work.

19. Viewpoint, Incomes Data Services, Report 640, May 1993, p1 This report highlighted that "employment in manufacturing ....is at its lowest level for well over a century ".

20. 'The End of Unemployment' by Charles Leadbeater & Geoff Mulgan in The End of Unemployment:bringing work to life, Demos Quarterly, Issue 2, 1994, p6.

21. Source: Henley Centre for Forecasting, Planning for Social Change.

22. The House of Lords in a landmark ruling in 1994 declared that more than 600,000 British part-time workers must have the same redundancy and unfair dismissal rights as full timers. The Law Lords ruling removed provisions of the Employment Protection Act 1978, ruling that the act breached European Union law on equal pay and equal treatment for men and women at work. The decision confirmed the right of the Equal Opportunities Commission to challenge British legislation as incompatible with European Union Law.

23. As cited before 'The End of Unemployment: bringing work to life' by Charles Leadbeater & Geoff Mulgan.p6.

24. Survey of Long Term Employment Strategies, Institute of Management & Manpower plc, 1993.

25. Men as well as women are increasingly doing discontinuous work according to the ESRC research centre on microsocial change at Essex University. In the early 1990s they reported that 25% of households experienced a substantial change - either up or down - in their income each year, and a third more households were receiving benefit than government figures indicated.

26. See for example 'Employability and Job Security in the 21st Century' by Rosabeth Moss Kanter, in the Demos Quarterly, Issue 2, 1994, p16-17.

27. Synergy data suggests that younger women are less concerned about financial security than men and women of the same age were 20 years ago. There is also a wealth of evidence of more women wanting to work part-time. The most common form of flexible working in the UK is part-time work which is undertaken predominantly by women. The UK ranks second in the EU to Denmark for its rate of women part-timers .Source: Families and Work, IYF Factsheet 3, 1994. See also Demos Quarterly, Issue 2.

28. Survey of Long Term Employment Strategies, Institute of Management and Manpower plc, 1993. This report indicated that at least 62% of firms aim to move away from traditional work patterns because of the need to increase productivity (23%); achieve cost reductions (23%) or increase flexibility (16%). About Time - The revolution in Work and Family Life by Patricia Hewitt, IPPR/Rivers Oram Press, 1993. This report documents the way the traditional model of full time, permanent employment is increasingly under challenge. It showed that

only one in three employees now works a 'normal' five day week with the rest working part-time, flexitime or at home. It is a comprehensive review of the history of traditional work patterns and the social, economic and technological changes which have given rise to challenges to this traditional way of working. It also included significant sections on the employment protection and rights more 'temporary' workers need for flexibility to work favourably for them as well as employers.

29. 'The End of Unemployment: bringing work to life' by Charles Leadbeater & Geoff Mulgan. This article points out that across the European Union three times as many full timers want to go part-time as vice versa. Jowell et al, 1991, British Social Attitudes - the 8th report found that 12% of male full time workers and 11% of female full time workers would like to go part-time if they had the option.

30. Attitudes to part-time Work: A report on Qualitative Research, April 1992, Department of Employment, British Market Research Bureau, see especially Chapter 4, p30-51. The report indicated that the three main drivers for part-time work were money; contact; self esteem. A number of women in the focus groups commented that they wanted to be financially independent - to earn 'their own money', p34. Many women respondents said that working part-time boosted their morale, raised their self esteem, gave them a feeling of worth and increased their self confidence, p38 The report commented that ......"younger and possibly more educated women, were more conscious of equal opportunities and career prospects.. They also tended to demonstrate more drive and enthusiasm."

31. The experience of British Airways is referred to both in Opportunity 2000's newsletter, Autumn 1993, page 1, and also in more detail in 'About Time - The Revolution in Work and Family Life by Patricia Hewitt, IPPR/Rivers Oram Press, 1993. Virgin's experience is referred to in New Ways to Work newsletter, October 1993. Virgin, faced with the prospect of redundancies, invited employees to take up between 3-6 months unpaid leave and to participate in a job sharing scheme.

32. For more information on this consult: The best of both worlds: Inland Revenue Factual Study of Working Patterns, IRSF, October 1992

33. Change At the Top: working flexibly at senior and managerial levels in the organisations. Sponsored by NatWest bank and published by New Ways to Work, 1993

34. Isabel Boyer, Flexible Working for Managers, Chartered Institute of Management Accountants, 1993. Review of the book, Opportunity 2000 Newsletter, July 1993

35. Chris Haskins, The Employers View, in Demos Quarterly, Issue 2, p 30-31

36. The BBC is currently reviewing its equal opportunities strategy and is already moving beyond workplace creches to more flexible ways of resolving child care issues. They hope to be expanding an already existing subsidised emergency nanny service which provides emergency cover when children are ill or when childminders are ill. The policy developed out of staff surveys which found that many staff reported in as 'sick' when in fact it was the child who was ill or child care arrangements had fallen through. The survey allowed them to recognise the business cost of 'absenteeism'. They are also currently considering other initiatives - child care vouchers, more flexible ways of working and elder care. Source: BBC. There is a wealth of literature on best practice in this area. For a range of company services see: UK Employer Initiatives: Working Examples of Family Friendly and Equal Opportunities Policies. A Parents at Work/Wainwright Trust publication, 1994. The Family Friendly Employer: Examples from Europe by Christine Hogg and Lisa Harker. Published by the DayCare Trust in association with the Families and Work Institute, New York, 1992. Changing Times: A guide to flexible work patterns for human resource managers. Sponsored by NatWest Bank and published by New Ways to Work, 1993. Change at the Top: Working Flexibly at

senior and managerial levels in organisations. Sponsored by NatWest Bank and published by New Ways to Work, 1993

37. American Express based in Brighton has set up a child care information and development centre, ChildCare Links which advises other employers in the areas as well as members of the public of the range of child care facilities on offer. It arose after they carried out a work/home survey and a series of focus groups for them to establish what the particular needs of employees were. It was set up in direct response to a recognition that fluctuations in productivity were attributable to lost work days because of employees' difficulties with child care arrangements and it was an attempt to help stimulate supply in the area as a whole. Other employers now fund the project. In business terms the costs of recruiting one new member of staff is much higher than the annual contribution to the project. American Express also reports that it has led to an improved image as a family friendly employer both by members of the public and the customers. Source: The Family Friendly Employer; Examples from Europe. Christina Hogg and Lisa Harker. DayCare Trust, 1992, p119-121 For a range of best practice in the area see: The Family Friendly Employer; Examples from Europe. Christina Hogg and Lisa Harker. DayCare Trust/in association with the Families And Work Institute, New York, 1992; UK Employer Initiatives: Working Examples of Family Friendly and Equal Opportunities Policies, 1994

38. Rheena Bhavnani from the Organisation Development Centre at City University and an expert in developing women's mentoring schemes within companies argues that many of the mentors as well as mentees gain enormously from the relationship.

39. Launched in October 1991, Opportunity 2000 had the public backing of 61 major employers.It now has 268 members employing 25% of the workforce. Source: Opportunity 2000, 8 September 1994

40. Corporate Culture and Caring: The Business Case for Family Friendly Provision. BIC/Institute of Personnel Management, 1993. This report broke new ground by calculating the costs of losing staff. The cost of losing a Deputy Manager at a supermarket was projected to be £29,5 89; the cost of losing a bank clerk was £5,252 (This calculation took account of vacancy & recruitment, training & induction, and tenure of service) If as Jo Gardiner, Campaign Manager, Industrial Society suggests this is averaged out, one arrives at the average business cost of £17,420 and from her conversations with recruitment agencies, she anticipates a minimum cost of £1,000 to replace any employee.

41. Charles Handy, *The Age of Unreason and The Empty Raincoat*. 'Change' by Charles Handy, Summary Abstract from a presentation at a Conference, The Future of the Family in Europe, Report by the WNC, Conference at Warwick University, 25-27 March 1993, p6-7. He refers to the notion that the glass ceiling will simply melt away through the process of delayering.

42. A forthcoming paper by David Cannon for the Seven Million Working Paper series includes previously unpublished research on the 18-34 generation of University educated employees, many of whom worked in major companies in the USA and UK. It indicates that a small group of companies are recognising the need to restructure and encourage employees to

cultivate other interests beyond work. Exit the Man in the Grey Suit by Marion Kozak, ChildCare Now, Volume 13, 1993 reviews recently published research from the New York's Families and Work Institute which found that the more family friendly and sensitive to other employee needs' companies are, the better their level of performance in the workplace.

43. Ray Pahl, (Ed) *On Work: Historical, Comparative and Theoretical Approaches*, Basil Blackwell 1988, p3. Pahl argues that the emergence of the male breadwinner, the collective mass worker and the very concept of unemployment and the unemployed only dates back 150-200 years and is now in reverse.

44. EOC Press release in April 1994. Jobs for the Boys, Analysis, Radio 4, BBC, 7 July 1994. Interview with EOC Head of Operations, Frank Spencer who commented that ...."I think the difficulty used to be in men's minds because there was plenty of work that they would traditionally do. Also, of course, to go into a female environment might have been off-putting to some men. We are now seeing a change. Those jobs that are there - men are going for them and even financial considerations are perhaps less significant than they used to be. .....I am talking about a wide range of jobs in retail, jobs in hotels and catering, clerical work, packing work, jobs that, as I say, are predominantly occupied by women". Also: Men Challenge for right to do 'women's work' by Charles Hymas and Lesley Thomas. Sunday Times, 20 February 1994

45. Information provided by Gerry Hassan, Demos Subscriber who has done background research for Demos on the Glasgow groups.

46. Attitudes to part-time Work: A Report on Qualitative Research, Department of Employment/Market Research Bureau, April 1992, p14

47. Maggie O'Kane, All in a Night's Work, The Guardian, 21 March 1994. This article is an excellent investigation of an unexplored area. Many women seeking male escorts are career women, and frequently married, often seeking company (and often sex) whilst on a business trip. The article also drew attention to changing attitudes to sexuality amongst women highlighting the growth of erotic fiction and the launch of the first female porn magazine. Similarly, Kaye Wellings et al, Sexual Behaviour in Britain, Penguin, 1994, revealed a new pattern of sexual behaviour amongst young women. 10% of women between 25 and 34 had had more than 10 partners, compared to just 4% in their mother's generation. Synergy data shows that career minded women are more in touch with enjoyment of their sexuality than other groups.

48. Naomi Wolf, *Fire With Fire*, Chatto and Windus, 1993

49. SuperWoman Keeps Going: Understanding the Female Web. A survey of Women's lives and expectations. National Council of Women of Great Britain, 1992, p9-10. Life At 33, The Fifth Follow Up of the National Child Development Study, ed by Elsa Ferri, ESRC/National Childrens Bureau and City University, 1993. They found that 70% of women disagreed with the statement ..."a marriage without children is not fully complete" as opposed to 62% of men.

50. Forthcoming working paper for the Seven Million project by David Cannon on the university educated 18-34 generation and their career/lifestyle expectations.

51. M Davidson & C Cooper, Female Managers in Britain - A Comparative Perspective, Human Resource Management, Volume 26, Number 2, 1987, p225.

52. From the British Household Panel Survey, published by the Economic and Social Research Council, 1994

53. 27.8 years in 1992, in England and Wales. Source: Social Trends, CSO/HMSO, 1994, p27

54. When one breaks down the Synergy data for women generally one finds that educated and professional career women of all ages are more willing than other women over 34 to experiment with their sexual identity. In tbis sense, they have set the trend for the younger generation of 18-34 year olds who as a group have become more attached to sexuality.

55. Kaye Wellings et al, Sexual Behaviour in Britain, Penguin, January 1994 A number of women's magazines like Marie Claire and For Women. have featured this as a growing trend. Synergy's tracking survey shows a similar trend among women in the 18-34 age group and more so amongst the 15-17 year olds.

56. Bowie, C and Ford, N (1989) 'Sexual Behaviour of Young People and the risk of HIV Infection', Journal of Epidemiology and Community Health 43, 1, pp61-65

57. John Balding, Young People in 1993, University of Exeter, 1994, For a detailed breakdown of the differences see p128-130

58. The research by John Balding cited above is reinforced by other educational research: Michael Barber, Young People and Their Attitudes to School: An Interim Report of a Research Project, The Centre for Successful Schools, Keele University, p6-8. This research was conducted via a database to probe the attitudes of 7,000-8,000 young people aged between 11-16 in secondary schools. This research took place 1993-94.

59. Charles Hymas & Julie Cohen, The Trouble With Boys, The Sunday Times, 19 June 1994. Charles Hymas, Women Edge out men in degree stakes, The Sunday Times, 26 June 1994. Hymas does recognise that men are still more likely to get first class degrees in two thirds of University subjects. John Authers, Girls Just Wanna Be Number One, Financial Times, September 3 1994. In this article he quotes figures from the Department of Education which shows that the proportion of 18 year old women attempting A levels is almost double what it was ten years ago (1982-1992). The proportion of men attempting A level only rose by 50%. Jobs for the Boys, Analysis, 7 July 1994. This included an interview with Professor Alan Smithers, Head of the Centre for Education & Research at Manchester University referring to the rate of change over the last ten years concerning male and female education levels. He was quoted as saying ...."In the last ten years, there has been a dramatic change. Girls began to move ahead through overall and GCSE. They are now doing better at A level and at University. Although they are still a bit behind with regard to firsts. Where you take first and upper seconds together they are doing better."

60. Michael Banks et al, Careers and Identities, Open University Press, 1992 p.129

61. Banks, M et al , Careers and Identities. Milton Keynes: Open University, 1992. See also Unger R and Crawford M , Women and Gender: A Feminist Psychology, New York: McGraw and Hill, 1992

62. Intelligence, Volume 8, Issue 4, 1993, Pensions Investment Research Consultants Ltd. Figures for women on the boards of the FTSE top 100 companies for 1993. Interestingly, they are overwhelmingly confined to non-executive directorships. Only six women occupy Executive Directorships.

63. National Management Salary Survey, Institute of Management & Remuneration Economics, 1994. These figures are quoted from this latest report (although this has been subject to criticism from companies and from Opportunity 2000). They surveyed 21,000 individuals in 339 organisations. Even if these statistics do not reflect the entire picture, previous figures indicate that few women fill senior jobs: standing at 3% of senior managers and 9% of the management population as a whole. Source: The Key to The Men's Club by Trudy Coe. Institute of Management, 1992

64. Source: EOC figures from 'Some Facts About Women 1994' and calculated to take account of the real pay rise they would require to achieve parity with men.

65. National Management Salary Survey, Institute of Management 1994. The average female manager earns £27,862 compared to an average male earning of £32,303. Women earn 13.7% less than men. In fact we have calculated that women managers would require a 16% rise to keep up with the average male earners.

66. Jo Gardiner, Women's Training, Career & Development Opportunities: Barriers, Initiatives & Agenda for Action. Industrial Society, 1993, p3. This document was drawn up after a number of informal breakfasts with senior career women and men. It is a distillation of some of their main thoughts on the barriers to women. 'The Key to the Men's Club' by Trudy Coe, Institute of Management, 1992. This survey found that 74% of women managers strongly agreed with the statement that 'women have positive skills to bring to the workplace', whilst only 35% of male managers strongly agreed. 18% of men and 12% of women admit they do, or would find it difficult to work for a woman manager.

67. The Key to the Men's Club, Institute of Management, 1992, p15. When were asked about the main barriers to their career, three out of the top four barriers cited related to gender bias: 43% listed the 'men's club' network as the main barrier; 35% listed the prejudice of colleagues and 23% listed sexual discrimination/harassment. Women's Training, Career and Development Opportunities: Barriers, Initiatives and Agenda for Action. Industrial Society, 1993. This report summarises in the form of bullet points the main barriers to senior women pursuing careers. Women's Participation in the Workforce, Institute of Directors, 1992. (The Institute of Directors surveyed 200 of their members). 37% said that lack of equal opportunities for women resulted from male attitudes towards women; 36% said they had suffered discrimination. 23% thought male prejudice was a major obstacle to career success. Source: Equal Opportunities Review, May/June 1992, p.4

68. Masculinity and the British Organisation Man, Michael Roper, Oxford University Press, 1994, p. 227

69. Once the fanfare of publicity surrounding the launch of Opportunity 2000 in 1991 died down, a number of articles appeared raising questions about the level of qualitative success the campaign was having. Anecdotally, disquiet has also been expressed. Gender Off the Agenda by William Kay, Mail on Sunday, 14 February 1994.Great Expectations: Assessing what Opportunity 2000 has achieved by Diane Summers, The Financial Times, 18 November 1992. Opportunity 2000: What Happens After Awareness? by Tom Nash, Employment.

70. TrainFair: A Survey on Women's training opportunities, The Industrial Society, May 1993 The report concludes that "relatively few women said they had access to career guidance and mentoring schemes, compared with the number of organisations claiming to offer them" and "concluded that there appears to be a gap between women's expectations of training and development opportunities and the practical initiatives offered by employers to enable women to take full advantage of them." The report also contains a number of suggestions as to how training can be improved.

71. The Key to the Men's Club, by Trudy Coe, Institute of Management Report, 1992, p4. The report contains examples of the gap between women's expectations, their needs and the lack of an infrastructure to realise them.

72. SuperWoman Keeps Going: Understanding the Female Web. A survey of Women's Lives and Expectations. National Council of Women of Great Britain, p6, 11 & 14.

73. EUROSTAT No 50/93, 1 December 1993. In its Women At Work section, the report comments that work is clearly influenced by family life, especially children. The activity rate for mothers 20-39 with at least one child under five is 26% below the rate for similar women with no children. In Denmark where child care facilities are well developed, the rate tops 80% for women 20-39 regardless of children. However in the UK which has the highest rate for women with no children - over 90% - the figure drops to 50% for those women with childen. The same report was press released on the basis of 'Conflict of Work and Home'. The Key to the Men's Club by Trudy Coe, Institute of Management, 1992. This report found that women managers were more likely than their male counterparts to favour greater government support for child care and 64% of women thought that tax relief should be extended to all forms of child care.

74. In a Business Matters BBC TV programme, Breaking the Glass Ceiling, 8.7.93, Trudy Coe argued that there was anecdotal evidence that male managers were threatened. See also her report.

75. The Key to the Men's Club by Trudy Coe, Institute of Management, 1992. p 22 and 20. Only 25% of women and 15% of men believe that their organisation should use quotas and 'some took the view that it was not the job of the organisation to provide help to employees.' For example an unprompted comment from a senior male manager: 'with massive unemployment we don't need to encourage women into the workplace'. Another participant said 'companies are designed to make a profit and provide a service to customers - not to provide extras for staff.'

76. Opportunity 2000, Incomes Data Services Study 535, August 1993, p12-13. For those interested in the reasons other companies have opted for targets consult the above report and also the following: Opportunity 2000, Equal Opportunities Review No 41, January/February 1992

77. Women's Participation in the Workforce, Institute of Directors, 1992. Survey conducted amongst 200 of the Institute of Director's women members. Other barriers identified other than male attitudes, included fewer opportunities for women in senior positions (33%); difficulties with women returning to work because of child care and flexible working (18%) and women's domestic commitments (18%). 87% of the female directors felt that women face obstacles not encountered by men with 35% identifying responsibilities to children as an obstacle; 29% argued that there was a greater need for career breaks; 23% referred to male prejudice; women not being taken seriously (21%). Of the 36% of women who had suffered discrimination, 42% thought that they had to prove themselves and work harder. The Key to the Men's Club by Trudy Coe, Institute of Management, 1992, p17. This found that even amongst women there was little support for a change in the law to allow for positive discrimination. Only 1% of men and 4% of women strongly agree with positive discrimination. 43% of men strongly disagree with it and 29% of women strongly disagree. The report also found that male and female managers were very confused about the difference between targets and quotas. 9% of women and 10% of men questioned talked about 'quotas' in their organisation when in fact they were targets. The backlash against targets may therefore be stronger than is already realised. p. 17, p.20.

78. In the Line of Fire, First Sight, BBC TV, November 1993

79. Women's Training, Career & Development Opportunities: Barriers, Initiatives and Agenda for Action, p.4 . Industrial Society 1993. Women's Participation in the Workforce, Institute of Directors, 1992. 42% surveyed thought that they had to prove themselves and work harder. Why Women Leave Senior Management Jobs: My Research Approach and Some Initial Findings by Dr Judi Marshall, Chapter in Tanton, M (Ed), Women In Management: The Second Wave, Routledge Press, 1994. This was a small group of eight senior managers who had opted out. All but one are back in employment, some in their own business.

80. M J Davidson and Cary Cooper: Female Managers in Britain - A Comparative Perspective, Human Resources Management Summer 1987, Volume 26, Number 2, p. 221-223 for stats. M Davidson & Cary Cooper: Executive Women Under Pressure, International Review of Applied Psychology, Volume 35, 1986. The stress of combined occupational and parental roles, a review of the literature, by Suzanne Lewis and Cary Cooper, British Psychological Society, 1983.

81. The Key to the Men's Club by Trudy Coe, Institute of Management, 1992, p3. 42% of women managers who have had a caring responsibility say that it has affected their career as against only 16% of men.

82. Why Women Leave Senior Management Jobs: My Research Approach and Some Initial Findings by Dr Judi Marshall, Chapter in Tanton, M (Ed), Women In Management: The Second Wave, Routledge Press, 1994, p4-5

83. Working Women: More Than Time for New Approaches by Linda Tarr Whelan, Centre for Policy Alternatives, Washington DC.

84. Women Business Owners Factsheet, National Foundation for Women Business Owners, USA, 1992

85. National Management Remuneration Survey, Institute of Management, 1994. This report found that despite recent advances the number of women managers and directors in the UK actually fell from an all time high of 10.2% in 1993 to 9.5% in 1994. This fall has occurred at almost every level of management (although there were some counter trends: eg womens salaries, though less than mens, increased faster, and the proportion of women directors remained constant at 2.8%). However these figures have been questioned by some analysts.

86. Fair Play for Women Factsheet on Enterprise, Department of Employment & Equal Opportunities Commission, 1994 More Women 'Crack Glass Ceiling' by Clive Woodstock, The Guardian, July 13 1992. A less recent statistic put the rate of increase of women running their own business having almost trebled over the last decade with the rate of growth of women entering self employment far exceeding that of men. Two other books which have analysed this phenomenon are: The Woman Manager by Marilyn Davidson & Cary Cooper, Paul Chapman Publishing, 1992 . Women As Entrepreneurs by Sara Carter & Tom Cannon, Academic Press, 1992. The latter found that half the women interviewed thought that women only banks would be useful for women entrepreneurs (in the US there are some women only banks).

87. SuperWoman Keeps Going: A Survey of Women's Lives and Expectations, The National Council of Women in Great Britain, 1992, p13

88. Putting Families on the Map,   International Year of the Family Factsheet One, 1994.

89. Familia Oeconomica. A Survey of the Economics of the Family by John Ermisch, Scottish Journal of Political Economy, Volume 40, No 4, November 1993, p357-358.

90. General Household Survey, 1994, HMSO.

91. 1991 British Social Attitudes data, IYF Fact Sheet 3/94.

92. J Brannen and P Moss: Managing Mothers: Dual Earning Households After Maternity Leave, 1990 , Review in Working Mothers Association newsletter, 1990.

93. Life At 33, (Ed) Elsa Ferri, National Childrens Bureau/ESRC & City University, p32-33. See also ESRC Research Briefing Life at 33.

94. The Second Shift: Working Parents and the Revolution At Home by Professor Hochschild, Arlie Piatkus, 1990. She identifies three gender ideologies - traditional partners, transitionals and egalitarians. See also: Women and the Work/Family Dilemma by Deborah Swiss & Judith Squires, Wiley, 1993.

95. The Transition to Parenthood in dual earner couples by Suzan Lewis and Cary Cooper, Psychological Medicine 1988. p. 477, p. 289-301. Dr Suzan Lewis and Cary Cooper, Stress in two earner couples and stage in lifecycle, Journal of Occupational Psychology, 1987

96. This figure has been calculated by Paul Gregg and J. Wadsworth of the NIESR and will be published shortly. In other work Gregg has argued that the rise of the female breadwinner has been overstated. He focuses on the disincentives in the tax/benefits system which are discouraging women with unemployed partners from working.

97. There has been an overall fall in the number of births to all teenage mothers as well as a fall in births to mothers under 16 years between 1981 and 1991 (Source: Parents and Families, IYF Factsheet 5, 1994). Irene Bruegel and Fiona Harris, School of Land Management, South Bank University is analysing the group of women who have had children early from data collected from the National Child Development study. What Makes Girls So Clever by Valerie Walkerdine, The Independent, 6 September 1993. Based at the University of London, she is conducting the third part of a longitudinal study of two groups of girls, one at 16 the other at 21. This shows that there is a huge attainment gap between middle class girls at fee paying schools/well funded state schools and working class girls at schools in poorer areas.

98. The Parenting Deficit by Amitai Etzioni, Demos, 1993, p30

99. Recent surveys suggest that families are becoming less willing to accept the major burden of care and that older people are less willing to depend on their children when it requires a long term commitment. Yet the pressures to care are increasing. In 1990, 6.8 million people in Britain had some caring responsibilities, an increase of almost 1 million people since 1985. There is currently only one benefit specifically for carers and only 17.5% qualify. Carers are less likely to be in employment than the population as a whole. Statistical and survey sources: Families and Caring, IYF Factsheet 4, 1994.

100. Henley Time Use Data, 1993.

101. Families And Work, IYF Factsheet 3, 1994.

102. Managing Mothers: Dual Earning Households After Maternity Leave by J Brannen & P Moss, cited above.

103. Peter Ashby of Full Employment UK has been conducting a series of focus groups with unemployed young men exploring attitudes to workfare. These focus groups confirmed that

this group were resistant for the reasons stated. He was interviewed on this subject on Radio 4's Analysis, Jobs for the Boys, 7 July 1994.

104. No Man's Land - Men's Changing Commitments to Family and Work by Kathleen Gerson, Basic Books, 1993

105. Attitudes to part-time Working. A Report on Qualitative Research, April 1992, Department of Employment. Research conducted by the British Market Research Bureau, p14 & p70

106. The Rising Cost of Exclusion, The End to Unemployment: bringing work to life, Demos Quarterly, Issue 2, p24-25. A detailed explanation of the background to the levels of unskilled unemployed young men. Danger: Men Not At Work (Unemployment and Non-employment in the UK and Beyond) by Edward Balls, Work and Welfare: Tackling the Jobs Deficit, IPPR/Commission on Social Justice, 1993, p23-24. "Young unemployed men find that low wage employment with poor future prospects is an increasingly unattractive alternative to 'non-market' activities...For example, drug use, informal economy and benefit fraud." Peter Ashby of Full Employment UK on Radio 4's Analysis, Jobs for the Boys on 7 July 1994 spoke about his focus group work and the dangers of a drift into crime for young unemployed men.

107. Equal Opportunities Commission, Annual Report, 1993. In addition to complaints about job segregation, men were also concerned about age discrimination with 6% recruitment complaints concerning this (especially affecting men 55+). 1% are from men complaining about discrimination when applying for part-time jobs. 24% of general enquiries are from men seeking advice about equal opportunities in the recruitment process. Frank Spencer, Operations Director confirmed to Demos that an investigation is underway. There have been several news articles over the last two years covering this issue.

108. Men and Women At Work, Link Up Services. 26 May 1993. This was a very small scale survey of 118 male respondents. Its data confirmed that men were more likely than women to have their sexuality questioned for applying for a job typically seen as 'women's work' by employers. Frank Spencer, Operations Director of the EOC, commented on Radio 4's Analysis, Jobs for the Boys (July 7 1994) that " they (employers) are discriminating against men ....it's a question of custom and practice and if they've traditionally employed women in these jobs, then it needs a shift in attitudes to open up those jobs to women".

109. Balding J, Young People in 1993, University of Exeter, 1994, p128-30. Barber M, Young People and Their Attitudes to School: An Interim Report of a Research Project, The Centre for Successful Schools, Keele Univesirt, p6-8. He argues that a major educational issue for the future is rethinking of equal opportunities to avoid male under achievement, especiallly given that poorly educated men are the most prominent group in the statistics. See also news articles: Charles Hymas & Julie Cohen, The Trouble With Boys, The Sunday Times, 19 June 1994

110. According to Sebastian Kraemer of the Tavistock Clinic, quoted on Analysis, Radio 4, July 7 1994. This figure is significantly higher than that for women in the age group. This is because women are five times more likely to take overdoses but five times less likely to succeed in actually committing suicide. See also: Review Article, British Medical Journal, Minerva, 1989 cites the figures for men as well.

111. Follett B, Closing The Gender Gap, Fabian Review, Volume 105, No 3. 43% of women voted Conservative in 1992 whilst only 34% voted Labour, one of the largest gender gaps to emerge though not for any obvious reason. Labour did however do well with women in the 18-24 age group with a 13% advantage over the Conservatives. In all others, the gender gap worked against Labour widening with age until it reached 20% with women over 65.

Research amongst C1C2 women voters between 25-50 also showed that their ideal description of a party was "caring, efficient, friendly, honest, reliable, stable and just organisation whose members worked hard to help fight unemployment and make ordinary people better off. Lovenduski J & Norris P, Why Can't A Woman Be More Like A Man?, New Statesman & Society, 3 April 1992. These authors, well known for their explorations of the gender gap in British politics conclude that women are more likely than men to vote Conservative though the reasons for this are unclear. Labour's Lost Voters: Southern Discomforts 3, 26 September 1994, Fabian Society. This research on ten focus groups (divided evenly between C1C2 men and women). They were all voters who thought about voting Labour at the last election but in the end voted Conservative. It found that many women still believe that Labour represents the working man, and that the Conservative party is more in tune with middle class aspirations which women value. Significantly it confirmed that C1C2 women voters who think about voting Labour often do not go out to vote.

112. Polling data repeatedly confirms this trend. Gallup, March 1993, 84% of women were in favour of government action to increase the availability of after school activities. Gallup, January 1992. 88% of women are in favour of government action on wider provision of nursery education . MORI, Jan-July 1993, By averaging out issues of concern to women and men, significant differences emerged. Women were more likely to prioritise the NHS and education and men to prioritise Europe and the economy.

113. Women and Politics, MORI, June 1993.

114. The limits of conventional polling in the case of women is well documented by feminists and others who recognise that whilst women have historically been less party political than men, they are involved in a wide range of community politics -campaigning against the closure of a hospital for example. Nelson B & Chowdhury N, Women and Politics WorldWide, University Press, 1994. This trend is not confined to the UK. A 42 country wide study concludes that the notion that women are not political is undermined by evidence of their role in community action groups and volunteer organisations. The report concludes that women's activism is alive and well, it is simply not part of the conventional political process. For more information on anti-politics see: Mulgan G, Politics In An Anti Political Age, Chapter One, p7-36, Polity Press, 1994.

115. For more details on experience from abroad and on the debate around quotas in the Labour party see: Lovenduski J, Will Quotas Make Labour more 'woman friendly'?, Renewal, Volume 2, No 1, January 1994. Lovenduski J & Norris P (Eds), Gender & Party Politics, Sage 1993.

116. Wolf, N, *Fire With Fire*, Chatto & Windus, 1993, p6-7.

117. Hutton W, Why Women Must Be Central for the Left, The Guardian, 18 April 1994. He argues that women, traditionally more conservative than men, are now being radicalised through their experience of part-time service sector work. The unions are becoming 'feminised' as a consequence and therefore the Labour party must develop a package of policies which will capture the votes of working women.

118. Mulgan, G, Party Free Politics, New Statesman and Society, 15 April 1994.

119. Democrat Deficit: Young People and the Parliamentary Process, British Youth Council, 1993. BYC Briefing Young People: Changing the Face of British Politics. One in four 18 year olds in the last election failed to register, four times higher proportionately than the rest of the electorate.

120. These two figures are derived from two sources. Nick Sparrow, Director of ICM Research. In 1994 using a specially adjusted recall method in data collection, ICM/Guardian polls found that 43% of people aged between 18-24 did not vote either because they were either not registered or did not go out to vote. John Curtice, Senior Lecturer at the Department

of Politics, University of Stratchclyde and co-author of the British Election Study 1992 comes up with a similar figure. 20% of 18-24 year olds were not registered to vote before the 1992 general election (OPCS figures). Reanalysing figures of those eligible to vote from the Lord Chancellors Department, he calculates that 27% did not vote. By working out the percentage of non-voters from those eligible to vote the figure comes to 21.6%. Therefore 41.6% definitely did not vote in the last election. He argues that the figures could be rounded up to 45% because the British Election Study, however thorough, is not able to take account of the transient nature of this young population. Research assistance: Angus Peetz, BBC Producer.

121. Ferri E, Life At 33: 5th National Child Development Study, ESRC/City University,NCB, 1993, p168. 20% thought that none of the political parties would benefit them personally. The authors argue that this amounts to a distinct lack of faith in conventional party politics with a higher priority being put on the environment. 79% said that "we should tackle the problems in the environment even if this means slower economic growth" and 38% agreed that "preserving the environment is more important than any other political issue today", p170.

122. See Bob Worcester, MORI data on environmental activism and links to age, 1994.

123. Banks et al, Careers and Identities, Open University Press, 1992. When probed about their attitudes to the parties, Labour was the most popular at 50%, the Conservatives at 30% and the centre parties at 6%, with a significant gender bias to Labour at this age, unlike older voters. Anti political sentiment was at its strongest amongst those on YTS and the unemployed and at its lowest amongst the group in academic education.

124. 1991 National Survey of Voluntary Activity, Volunteer Centre UK, 1992. The other group with the fastest rate in volunteering is the 45-64 age group.

125. ESRC Briefing 4, Career and Identities, 1992.

126. Banks et al, Careers and Identities, Open University Press, 1992, p128-129. The same data (and other data on attitudes to employment training, education, home life and leisure) is published in ESRC Research Briefing No 4: Careers & Identities.

127. What Women Really Think, The Guardian, 7 March 1991.

128. Womens Voices: A Polling Report, Ms Foundation for Women & Centre for Policy Alternatives, September 1992, p10-11, p31. The distance is not as striking. 62% viewed the women's movement favourably but were distanced from the term feminist and the report argues that the women's movement 'needs to build coalitions with organisations where 65% of women are already active: their religious institutios, parent groups and community organisations.'

129. Naomi Wolf, *Fire with Fire*, p.64 The Age of Post Feminist Woman, Mail in Sunday, May 1988 quoting NOP research amongst women aged between 18-34 found that 28% would never describe themselves as feminist and 24% said they found feminism alienating. It also showed however that although 63% would call themselves feminist sometimes, only 9% would do so all the time.

130. Griffin C, I'm Not a Women Libber but.....', Feminism, Consciousness and Identity, The Social Identity of Women (Ed) Skevington S & Baker D, Sage 1989, p189-191. Pilcher J, I'm Not a Feminist, but...', Sociology Review, November 1983, p4-6. Dr Hafner J, The Choice of the New Generation, Feminism Now, Cosmopolitan Special Supplement, October 1993 (This explores the paradox of the way women are wary of the label feminist but value equal rights and indeed many of the arguments of the women's movement and it also explores who are the 'feminist' role models now.)

131. Dr Sianne G, Gender, Sex and Sexuality: Contemporary Psychological Perspectives, Taylor and Francis, 1994. This will be explored in more depth in a forthcoming paper by Dr Gerda Sianne for the Seven Million Working Paper series.

132. Banks et al, Careers and Identities, Open University Press, 1992, p128-129

This research confirmed that sex differences in the expression of sexuality between young women and young men were being eradicated.

133. Faludi S, *The Undeclared War Against Women*, Chatto& Windus, 1992. French M, *War Against Women*, Hamish & Hamilton, 1993

134. Crichton M, Disclosure, Arrow, 1994

135. Warren Farrell, *The Myth of Male power*, 4th Estate, 1994.

136. Thomas D, Not Guilty - Men: The Case for the Defence, Weidenfield & Nicholson, 1992. Lyndon N, No More Sex Wars, Sinclair:Stevenson, 1992

137. Dr Elliott M, Female Sexual Abuse: The Ultimate Taboo, Longman, 1993. Mother Madonna Whore, Estella Weldon, Guildford Press. Mother Love, BBC2, May 1994.

138. There have been various programmes and books drawing attention to both issues: First Sight, BBC TV, 1994 - Male victims of domestic violence. Mother Love BBC2- on female sexual abuse plus books such as Female Sexual Abuse: The Ultimate Taboo by Dr. Michele Elliott.

139. Dr Sianne G, Gender, Sex and Sexuality: Contemporary Psychological Perspectives, Taylor & Francis, 1994. Forthcoming Seven Million Working Paper by the author. The survey found that men have similar views to women with regard to their attitudes to feminism. They were however expressed with greater strength. Only 16% were unsympathetic to the aims of the movement but 90% made extended comments and 56% of these were negative.

140. Maxwell Magnus S, Keeping Mum, The Guardian, 22 June 1994

141. Pahl R (Ed), On Work: Historical, Comparative and Theoretical Approaches, Basil Blackwell, 1988, p3

142. Etzioni A, The Parenting Deficit, Demos, 1993, p12 and 29. He recommends that parents should spend where possible four hours a week at child care centres and that parents staying at home for two years should have ' incentives' - for example, vouchers to plough back into further education.

143. Albery N & Mezey M (Eds), Reinventing Society, Institute for Social Inventions, p17. The Dublin Community Mothers programme involves an experienced mother volunteering to visit a new mother as a 'formal friend' on a monthly basis for the first year of a baby's life. A study on the scheme found that those who had a community mother fared substantially better off and the babies were better cared for physically and educationally. This mentoring principle could be extended to be gender neutral and could also serve to link generations.

144. Albery N & Mezey M (Ed), Reinventing Society, Institute for Social Inventions, p26. A scheme along these lines has been operating in Germany involving boys working in hospitals, schools and nursing homes which could otherwise not afford enough staff. This allows for an insight into working life before making career choices, shows the premium placed on caring by society and creates self esteem. They are paid for their work though not at the market rate.

145. Faye Rice, How To Make Diversity Pay, Fortune Magazine, August 8 1994. The article referred to research findings which indicate that diverse teams of business students were more innovative and lateral in their approach to problems than all white business students. The business case for diversity is increasinglybeing stressed in the USA because of demographic trends. The US Labour Department's Workforce 2000 report showed that there would be dramatic demographic shifts in the US workforce by the next millenium. Nearly 85% of the 25

million entering the labour pool will be women, minorities or immigrants. There is a similar demographic trend in the UK though not as extreme.

146. A forthcoming Demos working paper by Rosemary Crompton on lessons from Europe will explore some of these themes in more depth.

147. Charlie Leadbeater & Geoff Mulgan, Lean Democracy & The Leadership Vacuum, p14-25, Demos Quarterly, Issue 3, 1994.

Other Demos publications available for £5.95 post free from Demos, 9 Bridewell Place, London EC4V 6AP.

Reconnecting Taxation by Geoff Mulgan, Director of Demos, and Robin Murray, adviser to the Government of Ontario.
ISBN 1 898309 00 0

An End to Illusions by Alan Duncan, Conservative MP for Rutland and Melton. ISBN 1 898309 05 1

Transforming the Dinosaurs by Sir Douglas Hague, Associate Fellow of Templeton College, Oxford. ISBN 1 898309 10 8

The Parenting Deficit by Amitai Etzioni, Professor of Sociology at George Washington University. ISBN 1 898309 20 5

Sharper Vision by Ian Hargreaves, Editor of the Independent. ISBN 1 898309 25 6

The World's New Fissures by Vincent Cable, Director of the International Economics Programme at the Royal Institute for International Affairs. ISBN 1 898309 353

The Audit Explosion by Michael Power, lecturer in Accounting and Finance and Coopers & Lybrand Fellow at the London School of Economics and Political Science. ISBN 1 898 309 302

The Mosaic of Learning: Schools and Teachers for the Next Century by David Hargreaves, Professor of Education at Cambridge University. ISBN 1 898 309 45 0

Alone Again: Ethics after Certainty, by Zygmunt Bauman, Emeritus Professor of Sociology at Leeds University. ISBN 1 898 309 40 X

The Demos Quarterly

Issue 1 featured Howard Gardner on '*Opening Minds*' and a series of articles on education. Other contributors included John Stewart and Amitai Etzioni.

Issue 2 is titled '*The End of Unemployment: Bringing Work to Life*'. Contributors included Rosabeth Moss Kanter, Paul Ormerod, Martin Wolf and Douglas Hague.

Issue 3, '*Lean Democracy*'. Featured articles by Geoff Mulgan and Charles Leadbeater on '*Lean democracy*' and a collection of articles on juries, electronic democracy and other future forms of democracy.

Demos

Demos is a registered charity. It is financed by voluntary donations from individuals, foundations and companies. The views expressed in publications are those of the authors alone. They do not represent Demos' institutional viewpoint.